Essay Hell's

Writing Survival Kit

Everything You Need to Conquer the College Application Essay

By Janine Robinson

Table of Contents

INTRODUCTION

As college-bound students set out on their quest to get into their top-choice schools, writing the college application essay(s) often will be the most challenging leg of the journey.

In fact, many students will be pushed into uncharted writing territory: writing about themselves. It doesn't help that most young writers are ill prepared and feel intense pressure at the same time.

A dull or off-putting essay can derail even the most stellar student's chance of getting into her or his dream school. At the same time, a bold and creative piece can help them push through the door.

In order to strike the perfect balance, students simply need to have some idea of what they are doing and why—and learn specific writing techniques to pull it off.

It's not that students don't have the basic language skills to write well, but most have never written the type of personal, narrative-style essay that helps them stand out from the crowd.

During high school, their writing experience rarely ventured into the world of personal, creative expression. Even those who wrote a lot of essays were chained to the traditional five-paragraph formula and encouraged to churn out the impenetrable prose meant to impress teachers and appease parents.

A New Style of Writing: Narrative

College application essays call for an entirely different style of writing. Most prompts for core essays—including The Common Application essay—are looking for what are known as personal statements, which are essays that reveal the essence of a student or what makes her or him tick. Above all, these essays need to be interesting and meaningful.

Along with schools that use The Common App, most major universities and colleges require personal statement essays for incoming freshmen and transfer students. They also are common for graduate and specialty school applications, as well as many scholarships.

The best personal statements use what are called "slice-of-life" essays, which explore and share one part of a student's life experience rather than trying to cover everything. The writing style is called "narrative" because it uses real-life stories to illuminate the writer's personality, talents, skills, experience and character. The structure is less formal; the tone is lighter and the voice is familiar.

To write these essays well, students need the confidence to push their writing comfort zone—to brainstorm original topics, share their poignant or entertaining stories and express what they value and how they learn. A little imagination and creativity can go a long way.

Take a Risk—Carefully

There's a lot riding on these essays, so it can feel intimidating to take a risk. But the real danger is writing an essay that is dull, predictable and safe. My advice to students is to be bold and daring, but to do it carefully. That means to try a new style, such as narrative writing, but first learn how it works.

Remember the Boy Scout mantra of exploring a new wilderness: "Be Prepared." See what other students have written in sample narrative essays, and learn the storytelling techniques used by writing veterans, such as authors and journalists.

Give these techniques a try, and see what works. Students will be surprised at the power of a good story, their story.

Most students simply need to learn how to wield the writing tools they already have. The Writing Survival Kit is loaded with the tips, strategies and techniques that will help them find and tell their stories, engage and connect with their readers, deliver meaningful messages and make memorable impressions.

Learn to Apply the Writing Skills You Already Have

In this guide, the advice is delivered in "chunks" of simple, clear instruction, which students will find easy to discover, digest and apply as they go. These instructions not only help students write better in general, they also teach how to apply specific techniques and strategies for writing personal, slice-of-life essays about themselves.

With these essays, it's time for students to wander off the beaten writing trail. They need to use fresh language to forge connections and seek deeper meaning; share insecurities, flaws and funny stories; explore the power of gray; play with words and ideas; use dialogue, sensory details and metaphors, even break the rules—as long as they know what the rules are and why they are bending them.

It's no longer enough to tell a story—students need to find their good ones and tell them well so they illuminate who they are, what they care about and how they learn. An effective college application essay must engage readers right away, and make them care about what the writer has to say.

Guidance for All Stages of Essay Writing

The tips and other helpful information are presented in the general order of writing a narrative essay—starting with finding a topic, focusing it with a main point, mapping out a writing plan, and using a variety of writing strategies and techniques to tell real-life stories and extract their meaning.

If students are still looking for a topic, start at Chapter 1. If they have a strong topic and rough draft, they might want to skip ahead to later chapters. They don't need to use all of these tools, but many can help them turn an average essay into a winner.

Students who are looking for more than essay writing tips and advice, and want a step-by-step guide for writing their narrative college application essays, should check out Essay Hell's other popular guide: Escape Essay Hell. It is the perfect companion to this Writing Survival Kit because it leads the writer through each step of the process, and shows when and why to use most of these writing techniques along the way.

This Writing Survival Kit, which is more of a "pick your tool and use it" when a student needs it guide, includes about a dozen sample essays. Students also can find an entire collection in Essay Hell's Heavenly Essays, which showcases 50 sample narrative essays, as well as an instructive analysis of each piece.

Everyone Has a Story to Tell

Although these guides offer additional writing support, there's a good chance the Writing Survival Kit will be all students need to craft their college application essays. These personal statements don't have to be that hard. All students need is a good attitude ("If other kids did it, I can, too!'), and to take the time to look back over all the experiences they have had up to this point.

They should stay open to offbeat, everyday or even outrageous topics, and pause to analyze and reflect upon what happened, what they felt and thought, and how they grew and changed. Then they can zero in on one moment or incident, and tap these writing tips to learn how to share it and reveal what they learned—about themselves, others and the world.

Above all, students should try to let go of their fears—especially those annoying inner voices that try to convince them that they can't write—and just take those first few steps. I'm confident they will not only find their way, but with determination and a little help, they will enjoy the journey.

Chapter One

PACKING THE BASICS

The most important feature of a standout college application essay is a strong topic. Most of this guide includes tips and advice on writing, but even the snazziest writing can't make up for a dull topic.

The tips in this chapter are intended to help you understand what makes an effective topic, and also help you find your own. Once you do that, you are off to a terrific start on your essay-writing adventure.

**Pick a Killer Topic**

Finding a unique and compelling topic is perhaps the most important piece of an effective essay. It is worth spending time brainstorming. Start early!

There are entire blogs and books about this process, but here are some of the best tips to get you started:

- Look for a "defining quality" or personal characteristic that you can showcase in your essay. Examples: logical, inquisitive, creative, competitive, leader…
- Mundane topics often work best: These are topics from everyday life: singing karaoke, dog sitting, designing T-shirts, riding busses, etc. Check out examples of mundane topics in the essays in Chapter 11: Being Slow; Dunkin Donuts; Christmas Tree Farm and Dreams.
- Don't try to impress: You don't need to feature your greatest achievement, experience or talent.
- Avoid laundry lists: Focus on making one main point about yourself thoroughly instead of listing accomplishments.
- Show your grit, which is your ability to confront daunting obstacles with raw determination. Look for topics that involved problems.
  Sample essays from Chapter 11 by students Sophie Funck, Max Rubin, Natalie Belyea, Raquelle Rubin and Alex Knoll all display grit.

Scour Your Past for Topic Ideas

Here are a few questions to get you started:

- Is there something about you that your target school would not expect to learn or know?
  Note: Here's an example: You are a computer science geek, but also love raising exotic beetles.

- Is there something from your background that helped define or shape who you are, or how you think, or what you want to change?
  Note: Not all students had an intense issue in their lives growing up, but those who have should consider writing about those experiences.

- Have you faced any obstacles or challenges that could have stopped you from pursuing something you cared about?
  Note: These don't need to be cataclysmic; often, simple ones from everyday life work best.

- Do you have any talents, interests, idiosyncrasies, passions, hobbies, obsessions, fears, phobias, flaws, or other qualities/characteristics that have helped shape you, or reflect who you are?
  Note: Do not rule out ones that you think are not impressive. These often make the best topics.

- What was one of the hardest lessons you ever had to learn?

- Have you experienced anything that changed who you were?

**Find Your Life Souvenirs**

Some of us are adept at scrolling back through time and recalling specific memories or "times" we had interesting experiences. Others (like me), not so much.

When asked to recall one of my most meaningful moments or incidents in my life, I immediately go blank. But if something sparks a memory, every detail will come back in vivid, living color.

So instead of trying to pull memories out of thin air, start by collecting those specific "somethings" that can trigger a memory. The idea is that one tangible, concrete object or piece of a memory often links to past experiences with larger meaning. These are a gold mine for real-life stories you can use as anecdotes (real-life mini stories) in your essays.

Here are the types of life souvenirs that might spark a story or topic idea:

- A shell you found while walking with your grandmother on the beach.
- A song you listened to while driving back and forth between your divorced parents' home.
- A dress you made for your first dance.
- A piece of metal you kept after you wrecked your car.
- A drawing you made while in the hospital for an operation.
- A bottle of hot sauce you kept from the chili cookout you won—or lost.
- A ticket stub to a special movie or other event.

Go through your favorite stuff, and search your home, room, computer files, social media posts, junk drawers, binder covers, closets, bookshelves, pockets, etc. Notice what you have kept—and why.

What do they remind you of? Often, you will discover a forgotten memory of something that happened. And suddenly, you have captured one of those "times" that can make the perfect anecdote for your narrative essay.

Discover a Powerful Story

When searching for one of your real-life stories to share in your essay, find one that illustrates the point you are making about yourself.

If you want to reveal how you are creative, you would look for "a time" you did something creative. If you want to reveal how you are resourceful, you would look for "a time" you did something resourceful. And on it goes like that.

But how do you know if the real-life example you found would be interesting enough to use as your anecdote in your introduction? Not everything that happened to you was compelling.

One feature almost always makes a story a story, and that's if it involved a problem. When talking literature, English teachers called this feature the conflict. The point is that if everything is going smoothly, there's not a lot to tell, at least nothing very interesting.

Once you think of a real-life incident or moment that was an example of your main point, see if it involved some type of problem. If it did, chances are that it will be captivating to read about.

Essayist and critic Phillip Lopate wrote: "Without conflict, your essay will drift into static mode, repeating your initial observation in a self-satisfied way. What gives an essay dynamism is the need to work out some problem, especially a problem that is not easily resolved."

Remember that problems come in all shapes and sizes. Here are other types of problems that can make an instant story: Challenges. Obstacles. Mistakes. Changes. Moves. Failures. Conflict. Arguments. Flaws. Weaknesses. Phobias. Hang-ups. Setback. Accident.

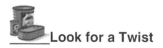# Look for a Twist

One of the best ways to pique your readers interest is to show or tell them something they didn't see coming. In writing, this is often called a twist, or a paradox or irony.

To the reader, these feel like welcome surprises. When writing about yourself, be on the lookout for your own personal twists. What is something we wouldn't expect to learn about you, or something unusual that happened to you? Was there something you were surprised to learn about yourself?

An unexpected feature is easier to recognize than to discover. When you have an idea for an anecdote or topic, check if it has an unpredictable quality—either the problem itself, or how you resolved it.

EXAMPLES:
- The time you built a computer and thought it didn't work—but it was unplugged.
- How you thought you landed the lead in the school play—because you always had in the past—and learned you got only a bit part.
- Why everyone thinks you are a wild and free spirit because you have crazy curly hair, but you are actually a perfectionist and almost OCD.
- How your dad owns several Dunkin Donut stores, but you hate donuts.
- Your entire family loves the ocean and water-related sports, but you can't swim.
- As the largest guy in your class, no one knows you cry at some commercials.
- The girl who was petrified of heights, but spent a summer cleaning high-rise windows.
- The baseball player who learned more sitting on the bench with a broken thumb than during his first three seasons as pitcher.

Free Write to Flesh Out Ideas

If you still can't find a topic idea, or have one and need related ideas and a focus, some writers do best to simply sit down and start writing. They might spend a little time thinking about the general ideas or concepts they want to cover, but they don't map it all out.

The idea is that the process itself of "free writing" generates fresh, new ideas. So they just start writing and don't worry where it's all leading. At the end, they review what they wrote, and extract out the best ideas.

Set a time for five or ten minutes, and write about your idea or yourself in general. To quote writing guru Natalie Goldberg from her book, Writing Down the Bones: "You are free to write the worst junk in America."

Don't worry about your grammar, spelling or punctuation. Try not to re-read or cross out anything. Let one random idea spark another. Some writing experts believe this exercise is more powerful if you write by hand on paper, but I think a computer works well, too.

Goldberg also instructs free writers to: "Go for the jugular. (If something comes up in your writing that is scary or naked, dive right into it. It probably has lots of energy.)"

With college application essays, if you have a quality about yourself you would like to explore, start by free writing about that idea. If you are a problem solver, start writing about that, and see where it takes you. You might be surprised that a whole new concept or direction might flow out of you, especially if you are digging for real-life moments from your past that you could use in your essay.

This doesn't work for everyone, but it is a powerful writing tool to get your creative juices flowing. It also allows you to find your natural writing voice, in that you free write more casually, like you talk, and don't fall into that stiff, formal writing that plagues high school English papers.

Chapter Two

SET THE COURSE

On any great journey, it helps immensely to know where you are going before you set out. That way, you will take the most direct route, as opposed to wandering all over the place or getting lost.

Having a simple writing plan and knowing the main point you intend to make in your essay are the two best ways to create focus and clarity for your writing.

Ditch the Five-Paragraph Essay

Most students were taught by their English teachers to use five paragraphs to write an essay. You start with a broad introduction with a main point (thesis), followed by three body paragraphs that support that thesis, and then a fifth paragraph to summarize and wrap it all up in a conclusion.

Stop doing that! At least not with your college app essay. Although you still want to have a main point that you are writing about, you don't have to state it in the introduction. Sometimes, you don't have to directly state it at all.

Instead, these essays are narrative in style. That means that they use a more casual, fluid format. Often, you start with an example of your main point instead of telling the reader what it will be. Then step through your other supporting points in the best order that makes sense, and usually this is chronological since you are writing about a part of your life.

A narrative essay has structure, but it's more like a winding path than a structured ladder with five distinct prongs. Your ideas still need to link together, and add up to making a compelling point about yourself. It's a more natural and loose approach to expressing yourself.

Make a Simple Outline

Even though the style of a narrative essay is more casual and less structured, you still need to map out what you plan to say and when you will say it. This doesn't mean you need an elaborate formal outline using Roman numerals and all that.

Just jot down the main ideas you plan to cover and number them in the order you want to write about them. In the first paragraph (#1) share an example of something that happened to you. The second paragraph (#2) could be about the background of that incident, or what led up to it. The third (#3) could be how you felt; the emotional impact. The fourth (#4) what you did about that incident or moment. The fifth (#5) explores what you learned. The sixth (#6) relates how you applied what you learned. The seventh (#7) wraps it up and projects into the future.

Sample Outline

1. Anecdote of a time something happened that illustrates your main point
2. Background (what led up to that "time")
3. How it made you feel
4. Steps you took to handle it
5. What you learned in the process
6. How you have applied what you learned to other parts of your life
7. Wrap it up; link back to anecdote; project to the future.

There's your outline. Then just flesh out those paragraphs with details and examples, and mix them around if you need to. The idea is that you break your ideas into "chunks" of writing, which you can then link together into one narrative that flows and makes sense.

 **Read Sample Essays**

This is one of the best things you can do to help you write your own essay. First, you can see the different, and often surprising topics, that other successful students have written about. Often, this sparks your own ideas.

Second, you can see for yourself the narrative style that most students use. If you study how they organized their essays, you can figure out how to structure your own. Look for parts that you like—a snippet of dialogue, an introspective sentence or two, or creative, sensory details—and use them in your writing.

The best artists steal. Or at least they "borrow" ideas and improve upon them and make them their own. Writers do this as well. This doesn't mean you should ever plagiarize, or copy someone else's writing word for word. But you can learn so much if you check out what others have written, and try to imitate what you like and give it your own flare using your voice, language and style.

Third, if you see certain topics used over and over, try to steer clear of those and come up with one that's more original or unique. If you are seeing them a lot, chances are so are the college admissions counselors.

EXAMPLES of over-used topics: Mission trips, sport victories, sports injuries, death of a grandparent, tutoring special needs kids, video games, etc. That's not to say these cliché topics cannot produce a winning essay, but students need to make sure they have something original and meaningful to say about them.

Check out the sample essays in Chapter 11. They are not perfect, but each one uses one or more of the tips from this Writing Survival Guide. If you want more excellent examples of narrative essays, consider the Essay Hell collection called Heavenly Essays: 50 Narrative College Application Essays That Worked.

Summarize Your Main Point

You can't write something well unless you have a clear and focused idea of what you want to say. If you don't, your writing will end up general, confusing and dull.

No one likes nailing down a main point. It's hard. But it will save you loads of time and effort. Ask yourself: What is the main point I want to make with this essay? For college application essays, you are usually asked to talk about yourself. So that main point should be the main point you are going to highlight about yourself.

Try to spell it out in one sentence, or two at the most.

Say you are writing about how you are a problem solver. Your main point should give that topic an even sharper focus. What type of problem solver are you exactly? You have to pick something that narrows it down and reveals what type of problem solver you are—as opposed to any old problem solving person.

Remember, your essay should showcase something about you—such as a defining quality. But it needs also to be highly personal and about you. So if you can figure out not only that you are a problem solver, but also how your background, skills, personality, and values make you a unique and specific type of problem solver, then you can sharpen the focus—and write an essay that paints a clear and intriguing picture.

Are you a problem solver who uses intuition to figure out a challenge? Or are you a highly logical, meticulous problem solver who loves puzzles? Or are you a problem solver who is most effective when finding strengths in your friends and putting together an effective team to handle challenges?

Know your point first, then figure out a plan on how to show and tell it.

 **Illustrate Your Main Point**

One of the most popular writing techniques used by essay writers is the anecdote. This is a fancy word for telling a real-life story, usually one that lasted only a few minutes and is recounted in a paragraph or two.

An anecdote is one of the most powerful writing tools, especially for personal essays. They are used to "show" readers an example of a point you want to make about yourself, instead of just "telling" or explaining it to them.

Anecdotes also usually involve some type of action, which makes them naturally more compelling to read.

Here's an example from one of the Sample Essays in Chapter 11 written by student Kaylie Monahan at the end of this book:

Wearing my turquoise-and-red beaded sandals, a braided headband wrapped around my forehead, tan fringy shorts, and an oversized brown shirt emblazoned with a multi-colored tribal symbol, I stepped out of my mom's car filled with confidence and joy.

My dark, freshly curled hair blew in the warm summer air, and as I marched up to meet my friends, I smiled and flashed a peace sign for fun.

"Who dressed you today?" said one of my friends, giving me the up and down inspection.

In this introductory anecdote, Kaylie gave us an example of the main point she made in her essay: That she was the type of girl who stuck with her unique personal style even though it wasn't always popular.

Since an anecdote draws the reader in with a real-life moment, anecdotes are powerful "grabbers" for the introductions of college application essays. If you want to write about yourself and one of your main qualities, skills or talents, just start by relaying an example of "a time" that illustrates it.

Chapter Three

SHOW THE WAY

The best tactic to find your way on an essay writing adventure is to help your readers see where they are going for themselves. Here are ways to "show" in your essays, which will engage your audience from the start and keep them reading through to the end.

Whether you start with an anecdote from real-life, or recreate an opening scene as in a movie, or entice them with sensory details, find the best writing device to pack action and intrigue into your essay.

 **"Show" Some Action**

Your essay is no good if no one wants to read it. All your brilliant ideas and insightful points won't work if you can't convince your reader to dive into your piece.

Writing experts advise students to hook or grab their readers with catchy first sentences. Those are fine if you can come up with something snappy enough. But often they come across as gimmicky, and have the opposite effect.

I like pulling the reader into your personal world by "showing" them something they can't help but want to see or watch. You need to make them care—the earlier the better.

Snag their attention with some action they can't resist. It can be physical (a rock landing on your car) or emotional (your drunk father locked you in a closet) or psychological (you were making a robot that could read minds) or intellectual (you figured out why structure is freeing in your poetry writing).

Show something that happened. Use an anecdote—a short example of a real-life moment or experience—as your introduction. Anecdotes "show" the reader instead of "tell" them about something that happened. Good ones are more like an example of a point than an explanation.

In Sophie Funck's sample essay in Chapter 11, notice how her anecdote in her introduction is an example of her topic—how she is "too slow":

As I walked into class, I spotted the two dreadful words on the white board before I even slid into my desk. They could have been in flashing neon lights: "Pop Quiz." Even though I had completed the reading homework, I knew I was sunk. My cheeks grew hot as I tried to ignore my classmates' pencils furiously writing down answers.

"Think, just think," I told myself over and over, trying to conjure the relevant facts and information. Even though I read the exact words in the same book as everyone else, nothing stuck.

Does this make you want to keep reading?

Start Like a Movie

If you start your essay with an anecdote, or include one at all, don't lead up to it by setting an elaborate scene or a lot of background. The idea is to start your description right before the moment intensified, or the pain started, or the excitement peaked.

This is how anecdotes draw in the reader—they put you right in front of the most exciting moment, and go from there.

Most movies start this way. The device is called in media res. You are dropped into an action-packed, tense or dramatic moment right at the start. There's little set-up; just a big explosion of trouble and drama.

You want to do the same thing in your essay. In as few words as possible, set the scene and then roll the camera. Zoom in as close to the peak of the moment as possible.

See how Emily Walton starts her sample essay from Chapter 11 by showing us a scene from her job working at a Christmas tree farm. Notice how there is no background or introduction to this scene; she just drops us right in the middle with her:

As I was in the middle of tugging another prickly Christmas tree out of the stack, I felt a gentle, yet emphatic tap on my shoulder.

"Excuse me, I'm looking for the person who decorated these wreaths," said the insistent shopper.

With a red ribbon in my mouth and sap-stained hands, I turned around hoping to discover Martha Stewart. Instead, I found myself facing a short, elderly woman in a full-length coat with a matching blue hat. According to her church nametag, her name was Ms. Charlotte.

Humans always want to know what's next—especially if it involves action and some type of problem. Leverage that impulse. Show them something they can't resist.

After the anecdote, take them back in time and give the background and provide context, which explains why it happened.

Here's the background Emily gave right after sharing the anecdote about meeting Ms. Charlotte:

She informed me that as head of her church's Christmas Decorating Committee she was looking for something "Southern and unique." Ms. Charlotte asked for several sample wreaths, and said if they met her approval, she would order 40 more.

The size of the order surprised me. This was my first time working at my grandparents' Christmas tree lot in Burlington, North Carolina, and I felt as though I was just getting the knack for picking out the best trees and keeping up with the festive, though hectic business.

One trick is to write out your description as best you can, and then see if you can trim off the first couple sentences and still convey the impact of the moment. Often, you can condense your description by trimming away words or phrases that you don't need for it to make sense.

These take practice. Read sample narrative essays that start with anecdotes and see how the writers put you right in front of the dramatic moment. By leaving out background, you create suspense and keep your reader wanting more.

Use the 5Ws to Craft an Anecdote

When you write an anecdote to use for your introduction, you are recreating a moment in real life. To put readers in that moment, you must provide enough details so they can picture it. Let them see for themselves.

Start with the 5Ws from traditional news and feature writing: Who, What, When, Where and Why. Usually you will only need a few key words from each W. The trick is finding the shortest way to provide the most information. Sometimes it's super specific ("Wednesday at 3 p.m."); sometimes it's broad ("a few days ago").

Ask yourself: What does the reader need to know to put them back in that moment? Leave out everything else. You can fill in the details later.

- The Who is you, or any other main player(s) from that moment: a teacher, a parent, a best friend…

- The What is the thing that happened: a rock fell on your head; you drove to your stepmom's house; you grilled burgers for your dance team…

- The When is the date or time: last Fall, freshman year, the first week of summer, right before finals my senior year…

- The Where is particularly important since we need to have a visual sense of the landscape: sitting on a rock, riding in a Ford pick-up truck, bursting through the kitchen door…

- Save the Why for later—after your anecdote, when you start to provide background and context and explain what it all meant.

Invite Readers into the Scene

When describing a real-life moment in an anecdote, you want to help the reader feel as though she or he was there with you. Often, it's just a few sensory details, drawing from the data provided by all five of our senses, which will bring the moment to life, and make it feel real.

Once you think of a moment to write about, try to remember details from what you saw, heard, felt, smelled and even tasted. The more specific, the better. Include only the tidbits that matter.

When describing what you would see, include some color, describe a shape, or name a brand. Was there music playing? Even better, a specific song? Were there related smells? How did you feel?

See if you can spot how student Natalie Belyea used details in her sample essay from Chapter 11 to help you understand what she was feeling during her first visit to an acupuncturist (I put the details in **bold**.)

Lying motionless, my body tensed up as I could hear the careful, yet **quick unwrapping of needles**. A **sweet older Chinese woman** in a **physician's coat** methodically shuffled through the **dim room**. The supposedly **soothing oriental music of bamboo flutes and wind-like percussion** only heightened my pulse. An uneasy rush of panic engulfed my body.

"Don't worry; you won't feel a thing," Dr. Lily offered. "One, two, three."

"Okay. I'm ready," I responded **while shaking**.

"Natalie, the needle's already in!"

Usually, in an anecdote you only need a couple descriptors to set the broad scene, creating a visual panorama using words: on a rushing river, in a new Honda minivan, in the check-out line at White Castle, on the lumpy couch in the living room.

Then describe what happened. Use power verbs (Natalie used "tensed" and "shuffled" and "engulfed" and "shaking") to show the action, and pop in a few, key sensory details.

Remember, be patient with yourself. These take practice.

Show and Tell in Your Essay

To me, this is one of the most powerful writing concepts out there. I wish I had learned it sooner.

We all have heard about the importance of "showing" in good writing. This holds especially true for college application essays, since one of the goals is to engage those potentially bored-to-tears admissions counselors from the get-go.

One of the purest techniques of "showing" in writing is called the anecdote, which I encourage students to use in their introductions. But effective essays also include quite a bit of "telling." And that's fine.

To both show and tell, you show the reader something, and then you tell them what it means. Or you tell them about something, then you show them an example so they get what you mean. (Some writing teachers call this the "what" and the "so what.")

Check out how student Max Rubin started his essay by showing with an anecdote, and then went on to tell the reader what it meant in his sample essay in Chapter 11:

(**Showing**: Anecdote)

When we pulled up to the McDonald's drive-through, my friend ordered the usual for our group: "Four Big Macs, four large fries, and four large Cokes." But at the pick-up window, I poked my head out from the back seat and told the server: "Make that three of everything, please. And add a bottle of water."

"A bottle of water?" My friend turned to me with a baffled look on his face. "Since when? Are you on a diet or something?"

(**Telling**: Background)

I felt a flush of embarrassment, but I just tried to ignore the comments and change the subject. Not many teenage boys have to watch what they eat. Most of my friends can devour almost anything and stay thin.

I thought I was like them and dined on junk food without a second thought until about two years ago. One morning in the beginning of my sophomore year, I stepped on the scale and was shocked to see that I was more than 20 pounds overweight.

In almost any effective writing, you need both. To keep your reader engaged, shift back and forth between the two—showing and then telling; telling and then showing, and so forth.

To use this approach, it helps to know the difference:

Showing = Details; Specifics; Examples; Anecdotes
If you want to "show" something, ask, "Can you prove it with an example?"

Telling = Explaining; Analyzing; Reflecting; General Points
If you want to "tell" something, ask "Why? What does it mean? Explain it to me."

In these shorter essays, you will show at the beginning with an anecdote, and then the rest will be mostly "telling" (with some more showing interspersed along the way) or explaining what it all meant.

As readers, college admissions officers are looking for how you find personal meaning out of whatever happened to you. This is one way they assess your intelligence, critical thinking skills, unique coping strategies and life philosophies.

Chapter Four

KEEP THE PACE

Starting an essay can be the hardest part of your writing challenge. But helping your reader to keep moving through your piece is equally important.

The trick is to not give the reader any reason to stop. Keep any bumps out of their road by maintaining a smooth flow, using varied sentence lengths, an authoritative voice, smooth transitions and these other writing techniques.

 **Write a Bad First Draft**

If you had at least one English teacher who understands writing, she or he must have told you at some point that writing is not an end goal, but a process. Must of us don't understand what this means until we try it ourselves with something we care a lot about—like getting into college.

No one, not even the greats, sat down and composed perfect prose in their first draft. That's not even a goal of writers. To produce wonderful prose, they had to pound out something bad or experimental first. For most of us, that's the hardest part. It can feel awful.

So you walk away for a bit, consume a bag of Doritos and organize your sock drawer, and think of all the million other things you would rather do than read that crappy draft you just wrote.

Eventually, you drag yourself back, re-read it, cringe at the bad parts, but surprise yourself that some sentences sounded not half bad, a few even pretty good. With new resolve, you start to make changes. Swap out a weak word or phrase for a better one. Switch around sentences to make it flow more smoothly. Chop out boring parts. Pop in a short sentence to break up too many long ones. Stuff like that.

There. You are doing it! The writing process. The beauty is that your second draft almost always will be better than the first. If it didn't work like that, no one would write anything, ever.

If you find some enjoyment from this tortuous process, you might have a promising career as a writer. Otherwise, just crank out an essay or two or twenty and get yourself into a dreamy college, and then pick a different career.

Stick to the Same Tense

I advise my students to always use the past tense when writing narrative essays. Sometimes it feels more natural to write the anecdotes (the short descriptions of real-life moments) in the present tense because it sounds more active and immediate, but the past almost always works better.

If you write an anecdote in the present tense, go through and change all the verbs to the past tense, even if it feels wrong at first. Then go back and read that out loud. It should sound better. Your anecdote will be consistent with the rest of your essay, which should stay in the past tense through to the end.

Once you have your rough draft and are done messing with it, make sure to go through it carefully and check if you slipped into the present tense. Just shift back to the past. Even moments that happened not very long ago need to stay with the past.

Go with Chronological Order

Many college application essays start with an anecdote or mini real-life story, and the writer often starts in the middle of the action. I love this approach. But where do you go after that? And how do you keep your essay flowing and make sense at the same time?

The best way is to stick with the natural order of events. Since you are writing about your life, the most straightforward structure is to go in order of when events happened. This will give your narrative a "spine," a basic structure, which provides a sense of continuity.

Say you started with an anecdote about "the time" you first drove a race car (your passion). You might start by describing an actual moment you stepped behind the wheel, or the moment you watched the speedometer pass 90 mph.

But where do you go from there? After the first paragraph, you will probably want to give some background or context to this mini-story. Take the reader back in time to one of your earliest memories or activities that first led to this passion for racing. And then trace it chronologically from that time, up through high school and to the current time of writing.

Of course, you will be developing your essay with reflective and introspective ideas and statements along the way to flesh out your ideas and main point. But if you get lost, go back and see if the order of your narrative follows the sequence of real time.

Of course, you will skip entire months and years, but stick to the basic order of significant events, and bring your reader along with you. "During elementary school…" "While working during the fall of my freshman year…"

Collect Synonyms for Your Main Points

When you write a personal statement essay, you need to have a clear idea of the main point you are making about yourself. This gives your essay focus.

Say you are writing about how you are a problem solver. Since you will be talking a lot about yourself with this skill, it would help to know some other words that mean the same thing, or are close enough.

They are called synonyms. Although English teachers often warn students against using a thesaurus, where you find synonyms for words, I think it can be a terrific help. Look up your word and keep a list of synonyms handy while you write.

Sometimes, you might even find a word that does a better job of expressing your idea or point. Synonyms for "problem solver" would be logical, deductive, analytical and resourceful. This exercise can help you tighten the focus of your essay and the point you are making about yourself.

You don't want to use a thesaurus to find "bigger" or more impressive words to use. If you don't know what a word means, don't use it. Find the best word.

 **Write with Authority**

Almost all narrative essays are written in the first person. This is when you speak from the point of view of "I" and "me" and "we" and "us."

Writing in this point of view can be tricky. How many times can you say "I" anyway? One technique is to shift from your "I" statement into a more authoritative voice, and make your points as if they were facts. These statements may actually be more your opinion, but you write them as though they were true.

EXAMPLE: I love driving race cars. They are not only exciting, but belong to a world of speed and racing culture. Those with the guts to step behind the wheel are some of the smartest risk takers in the world.

Make sure not to shift into the second person: "You." Sometimes it might feel as though there is no other way to say something without using "you," but you usually can write around it. Often, saying "people" or "others" or general descriptions of the "you" will work.

Note: I use "you" often in this guide because it's not a personal essay. Instead, I am speaking to and about you, my reader, as opposed to telling you about myself.

Mix Up Sentence Lengths

When you are pounding out your rough draft, don't worry too much about your sentences. But when you go back to self-edit, look for (or create) variety in sentence lengths.

If you have a lot of long ones in a row, try to break some of them into shorter ones. Or pop in a short sentence to break them up. Your reader will thank you.

Short sentences not only keep the reader moving through your piece, but they show a confidence in your style. To craft a short sentence, you must be sure of your point. Long sentences that drone on reveal a lack of clarity and purpose.

A good way to see if a sentence is too long is to read it out loud. If you find yourself running out of breath before you reach a period, ~~and you have crammed too many points into it, which makes it hard to digest and monotonous to read~~, make sure to cut that one down. (See how I did that?)

Don't Force "Big" Words

Here's my rule for all those long, impressive SAT vocabulary words you learned so well in high school: If you don't use them when you talk to your friends and family, don't force them into your essay.

You know the ones I'm talking about: cacophony, plethora, deleterious, obsequious, multitudinous... If you find yourself wanting to use a few of these types of words because you do know them and they feel like the right word, sprinkle them sparingly throughout your essay. A few go a long way.

The key is to try to find the best word, and not the impressive word. Unlike a lot of English teachers, I encourage students to use their thesaurus to find alternative words. See what other words mean the same thing, or something similar.

However, do not pick the synonym that is the longest or sounds impressive. This is such a common error, and it bugs the heck out of admissions folks. Use the synonym that is the most representative of what you want to say.

Don't just trust me on this. One of author George Orwell's famous writing tips is, "Never use a long word when a shorter one will do."

Smooth Out Transitions

Nothing quashes the conversational style, tone and voice of a narrative essay more than those clunky transition words we all pulled out only for English assignments. There are betters ways to shift gears in your essay than using "hence" or "therefore" or "nevertheless."

A lot of times, you just don't need those words. Take them out and see if the transition still works.

What you want are words that link your points and ideas together so that the entire piece has a nice flow. One trick I like is to find words that mean the same thing (yes, I'm talking about synonyms) and use them as links in your narrative chain.

If you were talking about your passion for sky jumping in one sentence and want to shift to another point in the next paragraph, see if there's another word or phrase you can use for this "passion." Maybe say "my obsession with feeling like a bird" or "this recent burning interest in leaping out of airplanes."

ANOTHER EXAMPLE of linking paragraphs with related words or phrases:

> (last line of a paragraph) …since the first day I was born, I knew I was **a bit different**.
> (first line of following paragraph) Not only was I **left-handed** and had crazy **curly hair**, but I had an **extra toe** on both feet.

See how "a bit different" links with the descriptors you use in the following paragraph? The concepts are similar, so they help connect your point, and also the two paragraphs.

 **Lose the Lingo.**

In your essay, always keep it simple. Even if you have expertise in something, don't shift into technical language. You will lose your reader.

Writing is about making connections. If you use language or terminology that is highly specialized, you will only reach others who speak it. The rest of us dolts will be shut out of the conversation. Remember, your essay audience is a diverse group of people from all imaginable backgrounds—who really want to understand what makes you tick, what lights you up or what stokes your dreams.

If you are a computer science expert, and want to share an experience you had in that world, use language that anyone could understand. If you can't help using a long technical term, make sure to explain (briefly) what it means in layman's terms.

It is not impressive to go over the reader's head. You can explain what you know and do and love without a lot of long, dull technical words.

If you aren't sure where the line is, pass your essay by someone who does not share your passion. Ask them: "Does this make sense?" or "Do you get what I'm talking about? If not, where did I lose you?" And listen to their answers.

There's no way to make a connection if the reader has no idea what you are talking about. You might even piss readers off. The most confident writers keep it simple.

Chapter Five

BOND WITH READERS

One of the most important features of a standout college application essay is that the reader connects with it. Once you bond with your audience, they will then care about what you want to say; they will like who you are and will want you around. (This is exactly what you want an admissions officer to feel!)

The following writing tools, which will help you strike the right "tone" in your essay, will help you find ways to connect with your reader. Use these tips to show how you are friendly, accessible, funny, humble and above all, likeable.

 **Write Like You Talk**

College application essays are more casual than typical English papers and reports. They have a loose structure and you write them using the first person ("I"). You also write in a more familiar "voice," which helps connect with readers.

Avoid trying to impress the reader by using big words, or formal transitions, such as "nevertheless" and "therefore." Instead, stick to language you would use when you talk to a regular person. You don't use a lot of slang or foul language, of course, but only include words and phrases that are common in everyday conversation.

If you find you wrote something in your rough draft that you would never say in the real world, take it out.

One of the best ways to "hear" how you normally talk is to enlist a friend to ask you questions about yourself and have them take notes (typing is usually the fastest). Even if they only capture snippets, these can be invaluable.

Some sample questions to draw out how you talk about yourself, your ideas and opinions:

- How would you describe yourself to someone who didn't know you?
- Tell me about one of your most important interests or passions.
- What do you care about the most in your life?

(Follow up all these questions with more probing questions: Why is that? Why do you think that? How do you feel? Can you give me an example?)

Your friend might not catch every single word, but with luck he or she will capture how you naturally say some phrases and sentences. These are pure essay gold—since you will hear your authentic voice in those lines.

Play with those very words and phrases in your essay, even if they sound like borderline slang or too common. This is your unique "voice" and it will make your essay more real and convincing to the reader.

 **Open Up to Your Reader**

Admissions officers, and readers in general, will care about what you have to say in your writing only if they care about you.

Award-winning film producer Andrew Stanton, who wrote the Toy Story movies, Finding Nemo, Monsters, WALL-E, and many other blockbuster animated feature films, says the first commandment of storytelling is: **"Make me care."** You can do this by creating pathos (appealing to the emotions) in your essay.

One of the best ways to forge a connection is to get personal. Let down your guard and show some of your feelings. Revealing your inner thoughts and feelings will make you more human and likable. It also shows that you have an introspective or deep side, as well as the self-confidence to be vulnerable.

But how and where do you do this in a narrative essay? It's easy if you start with an anecdote that sets out some type of problem.

Once you describe the problem, conflict, obstacle, challenge, failure or mistake, you have the perfect opening to express how it made you feel. Share your thoughts and feelings from that moment using dialogue or quoting what went through your mind at the time.

When trouble hits, we usually have a moment, or a period of time, when it brings us down, makes us panic or worry, or simply ache. The idea is to help the reader understand and feel that low moment—but not dwell or whine or be pitiable.

Since everyone has experienced these similar emotions at some time, your reader will be much more likely to connect and empathize with you—and find it interesting how you worked it all out. Readers only can understand the significance of your upswing if they first get where you started.

Maintain Your Youthful Vibe

College admissions officers expect essays to be written by students. If yours sounds as though it was written by an adult, then they will suspect it was not your own work.

Here are some red flags that a too-helpful adult got their hands on your essay:

- The essay has a dense, formal structure and style.
- The writer uses too many long sentences and confusing, technical words.
- The essay is packed with elaborate references to specific accomplishments, which tend not to support the main point of the piece.
- The essay has references that are from a different generation, such as citing T.V. shows, movies, books or magazines that mainly adults enjoy. In general, stick with modern day culture from your own life, not your parents. (Example: Instead of comedian Jay Leno or David Letterman, it would be Jimmy Kimmel or Jon Stewart. Instead of Facebook and Twitter; Tumblr and Snapchat.)
- The essay is general and dull because it does not share a lot of personal points. Adults tend to take out anything they think "goes too far" and blanderize essays.
- The essay does not reflect a youthful voice or include vernacular from the millennial generation. Take out words you would not use when talking with your friends.

  If your essay is free from these pitfalls, it will more accurately reflect your true personality and character.

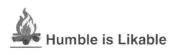 **Humble is Likable**

One of the easiest ways to make sure you are likable in your essay is to not give the reader reasons to dislike you. Resist the urge to try to impress the reader. Stay humble, especially when talking about your strengths, interests, talents and accomplishments.

Instead, "show" the reader by telling a real-life story (anecdote) about something that happened, and then go onto explain what you learned from it. Don't try to make it any more than it was. Focus more on what you did, what you learned, what you thought and what you believed.

Stay clear of listing accomplishments, throwing around smart-sounding concepts or language and the urge to mention how you are better than others. Your winning qualities should speak for themselves if you depict what happened well.

Instead of stating how you are a problem solver who uses insight to work out complex challenges, give an example of a time you did this. That way, you avoid the danger of sounding boastful or full of yourself. Let readers decide whether it's funny or not on their own.

Another way to endear yourself to the reader is to show vulnerability. Don't be afraid to admit a mistake, or reveal a flaw or confess a weakness. No one expects you to know everything. As long as you include your desire to keep learning and improve yourself, you will sound both humble and likable.

Here's another general tip for striking the right tone: If something is impressive, downplay it. If it is subtle or understated, give it a little more juice.

EXAMPLE of something impressive played down: "I was shocked to win first place at the competition."

EXAMPLE of something subtle played up: "Who would have thought my bee-keeping hobby would become a hot trend at my school?"

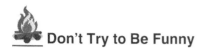 **Don't Try to Be Funny**

Humor can go a long way in making an essay entertaining and memorable. Some of the best college application essays have funny parts to them. Who doesn't like to laugh? But the humorous ones that worked were always those where the writer wasn't trying to be funny.

Instead, she or he related a real-story or incident (anecdote) that just happened to be funny. There's a huge difference.

Also, take your cue from the prompt. Some almost beg for creativity, imagination and a little fun. The University Of Chicago is famous for its irreverent prompts. One from several years ago asked students: "So, where is Waldo, really?"

If you are sharing something that happened to you, and it had some type of twist or irony to it, chances are it might elicit a giggle or laugh from your reader. And that's fine.

Don't embellish your description to get that response. Focus on telling the story in a straight, direct fashion.

Here's an example of a humorous anecdote from the introduction of a sample essay written by student Dylan Somerset, who is attending Boston University, from Heavenly Essays: A Collection of 50 Narrative College App Essays:

Standing by the display window, I wrapped my arms around Sarah's slippery waist, struggling as I pulled the sheer, black turtleneck over one arm. As I yanked the sweater over her other arm, I heard a snap. One of her fingers dropped to the ground.

Although Sarah and the store's other two mannequins were both relatively new, it has always been a battle to constantly change the mannequins and keep them fashionable. Needless to say, I was not looking forward to the skinny jeans.

Notice how Dylan wasn't necessarily trying to be funny, but she simply recounted a moment that was humorous. A subtle, but important difference.

Some of the best personal anecdotes spring from those family stories your parents or friends liked to recount over the years, or a moment you couldn't wait to tell your friends about. Remember the time you…?

There are specific types of humor that you can test out, such as sarcasm (when you say the opposite of what you mean) or self-deprecating humor.

Here's an example of an introduction from a Heaven Essays sample written by student Paige Greenwood, who is attending the University of San Francisco. She wields self-deprecation when she pokes fun of her body shape:

A disease plagues every member of my family: Greenwood hips. Scrolling through my father's vast collection of pictures ranging from baby photos to recent family vacations, I realized I had developed this dominant gene. I stared closely at a photo of my uncle, my father, my brother and I lined up on the shores of Hawaii and found that the wide hips on my torso mirrored those of my other family members. I was shocked.

Look for the humor or entertainment value in other sample essays you read. And see how the students presented their story, and what made it funny. If done right, you wouldn't notice they were trying.

Chapter Six

DIG DEEP

What's the point of a challenging adventure if you don't get anything out of it? In your narrative essay, share something that happened, usually with an anecdote. Now you need to help the reader understand why it mattered to you.

These writing tools will help you explore and explain in your essay the meaning of what happened. This will give your essay depth and show the reader how you think, and your ability to analyze and reflect.

Explain Meaning by "Telling"

Even though most narrative essays start with some type of real-life moment or incident (anecdote), they are more than recounting an entertaining story. The point is to share a story in order to examine what it meant to you, and what you learned from it.

The anecdote or mini-story will usually only take up the first part of your essay; the rest is all what you have to say about what it meant, its significance. This is when you get to reveal how you think, what you care about and how you learn.

After you engage your reader with an anecdote—which illustrates the point you want to make about yourself in the essay—it's time to go on and explain what it all means and why it matters to you and others.

One way to bring depth to your analysis is to reflect on what happened. Here are some lines that might help you share your thoughts and ideas:

"When I look back, I now realize…."
"Years later, I now believe…"
"It took me a while, but I now suspect that…"
"When I explored the events that led up to that day, I often think…"
"On another level, I now view it…"
"It caught me by surprise, but I now understand that…"
"After while, I started to think about all that I learned…"
"In some ways, I changed…"

You shared something that happened. That was "showing." After that, your essay is all about explaining—"telling"—what it meant.

Reveal Your Intellectual Vitality

Once you pick a point you want to make about yourself, and have found an anecdote to illustrate that point, you need to explain why it matters. To you. To others. And to the world in general.

Once you start to share your thoughts about what happened, you can take your points even deeper by asking "Why?"

Take a look at some of the points you have made in your rough draft, and ask yourself:

- "What about it?"
- "Why should you care?"
- "And that means what?"
- "Is that important?"
- "Why is that?"

These questions can help you flesh out or develop your essay and take it beyond just talking about something that happened, or what you did about it. They reveal your ability to think critically, and learn from experience.

Remember, you don't need all the right answers for these questions. Just offer your thoughts, ideas or best guesses. In general, these essays are a way to throw out some ideas, chew on them, kick them around, examine them from different angles and come up with conclusions.

The ability to take a simple incident or personal quality and examine and analyze it to find meaning reveals what is called "intellectual vitality." It's a sophisticated way to say thinking— and the best colleges can't get enough of it.

Look for Metaphors and Other Comparisons

A metaphor is when you draw a comparison of one object or action to another. One represents the other: "The trapdoor of depression."

Writers use them to help the reader understand a point that is more abstract in nature by comparing it to something tangible and concrete.

If you use a simile, you say it's "like" something else. If you use a metaphor, you say it "is" that thing. No matter the literary term; both compare one thing to another. In general, metaphors pack more punch than similes.

You do not need to force a metaphor into your essay to make it meaningful or impressive. But if you include one, it can demonstrate how you think on a more complex level and handle figurative (the opposite of literal) concepts.

For example, if you wrote your essay about the first time you learned to drive a stick shift, you have a chance to notice how some of the rules of driving reflect those in your life—and in all life (which makes it a universal truth, too.)

Like how we all start in first gear, slowly and often with a few jerks and grinds (in the car and in life). And how the ride smoothes out once we move into the higher gears on the highway (in the car and in life). Or how there are times you have no choice but to slam on the brakes in order not to crash (in the car and in life). With comparisons like this, you can broaden and deepen the description of your car ride experience into the metaphorical ride of life.

Often, you will notice how a smaller life event translates to a larger life lesson. Check out your anecdote and see if what you learned from that single experience also applies to other parts of your life.

If you find "life" comparisons in the experiences and concepts you share in your essay, you reveal the intellectual ability to find, shape and create meaning. Colleges love this.

The best rule for metaphors or other comparison techniques, such as similes, is to use only those you have never heard before. Otherwise, they are called clichés, which you should avoid.

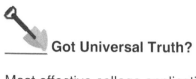 **Got Universal Truth?**

Most effective college application essays showcase a moment or experience that helped define who you are, or what sets you apart from others. In the process, writers usually share what they learned.

Often, you can extend what you learned about yourself and others into larger life lessons, which are called universal truths. This is another way a strong essay will connect with readers—it taps something that is true for everyone.

If you wrote about how you are a problem solver, and shared the time that you confronted some type of challenge using an imaginative solution, you learned how to solve that one issue. Like the time you used an old lawnmower engine to fix your parent's car.

Along the way, chances are you learned a larger lesson about how the world works (for everyone). It could be as simple as: What I learned is that if you get creative you can solve almost all your car problems. Now replace "car" with "life" and you will have a universal truth: If you get creative you can solve almost all your "life" problems.

To see if your lesson involved a universal truth, just put "in life" when you state what you learned.

EXAMPLE: I learned that to drive safely (in life), I need to pay attention to the warning signs (in life).

Chapter Seven

FIRE IT UP

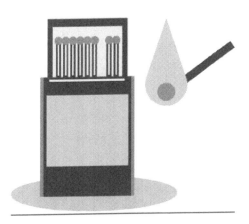

There's nothing worse than a boring experience. Everyone wants out. The same goes with these college application essays. They need to be exciting to read, otherwise, what's the point?

Here are some of the most powerful writing tools in this book that will help you make your essay impossible to stop reading. Use your topic choice, a snappy introduction, juicy details and other language devices to hook readers at the start, and hold their interest through to the end.

Take a Risk—Carefully

You have more to lose with these essays if you write a dull one than if you take a chance and write something more "out there." A bolder essay also is more likely to help you get into a school than keep you out—even though it is a risk you take.

Bold does not need to be shocking or scandalous. Often, the best way to be daring in writing is to express the truth simply and directly, focus on the details and be open and sincere.

If you think you have a unique or out of the box topic or story to tell, at least give it a shot. Write it out and you will know pretty quickly if it works or not. If in doubt, show it to someone whose opinion you value, someone who might have the same sensibility as an admissions counselor.

Even if you have a topic that is controversial or sensitive, don't let anyone talk you out of giving it a try. It almost always comes down to how you write about it and what you have to say.

If your topic is potentially upsetting or provocative, make sure to handle that part delicately, and don't go into too much detail. Let the most intense part hang in the background. Spend your time on what it all means.

Famous writing coach Roy Peter Clark has a writing rule: "Know when to back off and when to show off." He explains in his terrific Writing Tools book: "When the topic is most serious, understate; when least serious, exaggerate."

Many students intuitively are drawn to a story or event in their background because it was so affecting and formative. Topics about death, illness, abuse, and other personal events often are highly charged and emotional.

They almost always make the most powerful and effective essays if handled correctly. Again, describe the drama, but quickly move into how it affected you, what you did about it and what you learned. Usually, if you start off your essay with a specific example that illustrates the larger issue, that will be sufficient for your reader to get the picture.

Look for Buried Gold

In the world of newspapers, editors and writers have a saying called "burying the lede." A reporter would turn in a story about something that happened. The editor would review it and halfway down the piece discover something that was far more interesting than what the writer started with—and advise the writer to rework the story, and move that more interesting nugget to the top as the "lede."

Essays often have this same buried gold—a juicy tidbit that is wasted lower in the piece and would serve as a killer anecdote.

Remember, the goal is to start with something that engages the reader. Often, writers think they started with something interesting, but along the way, they included something even more interesting that they didn't notice. Sometimes, it takes someone else to point that out, like an editor.

Here is an example of a buried lede in a sample essay from Heavenly Essays, written by a student who is attending Middlebury College:

Being a religious teenager in a highly secular place can be difficult. Sometimes I have to admit I dread the cliché questions of friends: What do you do when you get sick? Why don't you go to the doctor? I can't believe you have never taken any medicine! But I patiently answer these questions and embrace this challenge because spiritual living is crucial to who I am.

For me, being religious doesn't just mean going to church every Sunday; it is a daily practice and supports a fearless approach to life. Although I may stand out in a crowd, and many of my peers don't understand my commitment to my religion, I don't compromise my faith. I have overcome countless scenarios with the help of prayer, including the biking accident I experienced while training for a 350-mile bike ride from New York City to Washington, DC.

(Buried Lede) Biking along Lake Washington, the trees flew past me and the wind whistled in my ears. The dry smell of summer filled the air, and my legs churned up and down. The wind was at my back, and I felt like I was flying. Seconds later, however, I veered out of control. My bike and I hit the pavement and skidded across the road.

This student's introduction was fine (hey, she got into a great school!), but she was telling instead of showing in her introduction. She could have started with the third paragraph, "Biking along Lake Washington..." and used that paragraph for her introduction. That anecdote put us in her shoes, and something happened—which draws us into the essays and makes us want to keep reading. We are concerned about what happened to her next.

Then she can tell or explain what it all meant, and use her original first couple paragraphs. All it takes is switching it up to put the drama at the top.

You can read your own draft and see if you started with something general, and check if you shared something later that was more specific, such as a real life example or incident, which would work far better for your introduction.

You have to trust that something that seemed minor or everyday at first could be interesting. When in doubt, give it a try as your introduction. Usually something specific works far better than a broad explanation.

It's particularly hard to spot your own buried gold. You can have someone else read your draft, and ask them if they see something in it that is more interesting than what you started with. If so, dig it up.

The Zen of Three

When you find yourself listing examples of points you are making, it's usually best to try to come up with three at a time. For some reason, that number has a pleasing balance to it.

- Lions and tigers and bears
- Beginning, middle and end
- Peter, Paul and Mary
- On your mark, get set, go!
- Red, white and blue
- Eat, Pray, Love

Of course, if you just have one example, use that. But it better be good, since it's a star by default. For some reason, two examples often feel odd; you almost want to divide them. This is not a hard and fast rule, but when you want to provide specific examples, go for three.

Four is a wash. It gets more traction if you take out one and stick with the trio.

EXAMPLE: Some of my favorite memories involve catching tadpoles at my grandma's pond, picking blueberries and jumping over mud puddles.

 **Name the Dog**

If you start your college application essay with an anecdote, or a short real-life moment, there's a trick to making that moment come alive for the reader. In his Writing Tools, Roy Peter Clark calls it "Get the Name of the Dog," and he means that often you can bump up your description if you provide more specific "concrete" details.

The dog is just an example. Instead of saying "The dog broke free from its leash and bolted toward the highway," try giving a more specific description of the dog: "The gray Labradoodle named Antoine broke free...."

When you give details, especially proper nouns (names of people, places and things: Larry, Yankee Stadium, Radiohead), you help ground the reader in your story. It's as though you are creating a video so readers can see what you are describing. Zoom in on the details with specific words or phrases to make writing feel more vivid, believable and interesting.

Even in the body of your essay, when you feel you are starting to get muddled in a lot of broad, sweeping sentences about what you think and feel, try to switch back to some concrete details. These will snap your reader back to attention.

Instead of saying you wore shoes, tell us the color and brand: "I walked onto the stage wearing my beat-up red Converse." Suddenly, we can picture you more clearly, and want to know more.

Example: Instead of eating cereal, say Wheaties or Cap'n Crunch. Instead of saying television comedies, say Seinfeld or The Simpsons. Instead of saying my sister, say "my big sister, Ruby Anne."

Go back through your rough draft and look for places that you can give a more specific description. This works like magic to spice up dull essays.

Pack a Punch With Power Verbs

The main place to use power verbs, also known as action verbs, is at the start of your essay, especially if you lead with an anecdote. If your anecdote is good, it most likely will describe something that happened. Some action!

Say you describe the time you first stepped behind the wheel of a race car. Instead of saying I "got into the car," use a power verb, such as "jumped" or "climbed." Instead of saying I "stepped on the gas," say I "punched the accelerator" or I "slammed my foot on the gas."

To spot places to slip in power verbs, go through your anecdote or your entire essay and find where you used "to be" verbs, such as "is" and "was" and "were" and "being." See if you can shift the sentence around and drop in an action verb.

If all you can think of is a general action verb, such as "to go" or "to walk," go ahead and check the thesaurus for other verbs that might describe your action more accurately, which will give your sentence more oomph. Instead of "I went to the ocean," maybe you "moseyed" or "skipped" or "sprinted" there.

You are not looking for more impressive or longer verbs, but ones that are more accurate and describe the action with more color and interest.

Essay coach Sara Nolan from Essay Intensive in New York City advises her students to use the Find/Replace tool in Word to check how many times they have used a word, and then find its variants.

Emphasize a Word by Where You Put it

I never found the famous writing manual The Elements of Style particularly helpful or inspiring when I was in high school. All those tedious Do's and Don'ts. The rules only started making sense once I started writing for a living.

Now, one of my favorite tips is the authors' point about placing important words at the beginning or end of sentences.

Example: After years of 5 a.m. practices and thousands of laps, I couldn't believe I was the only swimmer who came in last. (See how "last" has a bit of a punch?)

Be wary of other ways to emphasize words in your essays, and don't be tempted to put them in italics, or bold, or stick in exclamation points.

Author F. Scott Fitzgerald said: "Cut out all those exclamation marks. An exclamation mark is like laughing at your own joke."

And never use ALL CAPS. Those only make you look like a weak writer. Use only your words and what you have to say to emphasize your points.

Chapter Eight

FIX IT

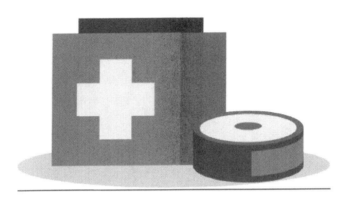

All great adventures have glitches or obstacles along the way. They wouldn't be true adventures without them. Someone stumbles, or even gets hurt. The trick is to recognize what went wrong, patch it up or make it better and move on.

For many students, the adventure of writing in a narrative style is a new challenge. Use the following tips, advice and ideas to keep your essay writing experience—and your essay itself—fluid and meaningful.

Back Up Your Points With Examples

In these essays, you may find yourself making broad, sweeping statements about what you think, what you value and what you believe. This is good stuff, but a little can go a long way.

The best way to rein your reader back into your essay is to follow up a general statement with some specific examples that help prove your point. This also is an opportunity to weave in more details about yourself.

EXAMPLE: I believe that it's important to embrace my weaknesses, especially my shyness. (Now back this up with an example.) Like the time I was mortified to talk in front of my class about my butterfly collection...

Go through your draft and look for places where you make a statement, claim or broad point and see if you can follow it up with something specific from your experience or background that supports it. If you can't, chances are it doesn't belong in the essay.

This is an excellent place for you to naturally weave in examples and details from other activities, interests and experiences from your life that will show how intriguing you are. These are especially significant if they were not mentioned elsewhere in your college application.

Refuel at the Halfway Mark

Let's assume you grabbed your reader at the start of your essay by engaging them with an anecdote. And after that you gave that moment or example some background to put it into context, and then you launched into what it all meant to you.

That's perfect! You are using the Show AND Tell technique that keeps your reader moving through your essay. You showed the reader with that anecdote, and now you are telling or explaining what it all meant.

One potential hazard in these essays is that once you kick into telling and explaining—which involves the world of the abstract and general—you might need to give your reader a break after a couple paragraphs.

My advice is to try to include something that shows again around the middle of your essay. Chances are you will start making assertions about steps you took to deal with your topic, and how it made you feel, what you think about it all. This is good stuff, but it can get a bit windy, if you know what I mean.

The best way to not lose your reader with too much telling is to pop in some of that juicy show material. Remember how you show? You give specific details and examples. You don't need an entire anecdote in the middle, just a few key nuggets of information that are tangible or colorful.

A good opportunity to shift back into showing in the middle of your essay is when you back up your points with examples (explained in the tip right before this one). A few concrete or sensory details, some proper names, some specific images, can revive your reader and snap them back to attention.

Then you can continue your explanation up until the end of your essay, where you ideally zing them with a memorable kicker.

Include Dialogue Correctly

A snippet of dialogue can bring an anecdote to life like no other writing device. If you are describing something that happened, nothing works better than bringing in someone else's voice—or your own.

If you want to work in a sentence or two from another speaker, make sure you format and punctuate it correctly. Here are a couple basic rules:

Every time someone speaks, start a new paragraph.

EXAMPLE:

It was dark when we arrived.

"I don't think we are in the right place," my sister said. "What if we are lost? I can't see a thing."

I grabbed my flashlight and kept walking.

"Someone's pulling my shirt," she said, and started to scream...

Enclose only the words the person said in quote marks. And include who said them. Usually you only need to let the reader know who said something, and resist the urge to include adverbs to describe how they did it.

Better to say:

"He hit me in the face," my dad said.

Instead of:

"He hit me in the face," my dad explained sadly and defensively.

Notice that almost all the punctuation with dialogue is "inside" (usually on the left of) the quotation marks.

If you need more help, Google "how to use dialogue" and make sure to get it right. If you don't, you have defeated the whole purpose of including it, since it will only distract from your essay and not enhance it.

If you want more examples, almost all the Sample Essays in Chapter 11 include dialogue, mainly in the introductions. You can also look in almost any published novel to see how to use quotations the right way.

Trust Your Ear for Language

When you are revising a draft, read it out loud and learn to trust your own response to words and sentences. If something sounds clunky, awkward, too weak or too strong, then it probably is that way. So change it.

Sometimes we are sick of writing and try to convince ourselves that something sounds good when it doesn't. You just want to be done with it. But if you want a good essay, don't kid yourself. Face the truth. Trust your instincts.

Tune your editing ear by reading sample essays by other students and notice when you like something, or when a line affects you (makes you laugh or cringe). Try to figure out how they did that or why it worked. You are developing your ear for language, and can start to listen to your own work in order to improve it.

If you aren't sure, test it out on someone else. If they agree, then you are probably on the right track.

Resist the Urge to Quote Famous People

As far as I can tell, quoting famous people rarely improves a slice-of-life essay. At best, it almost always sounds as though you needed something credible to beef up an essay. At worst, it sounds like you dropped one in because you thought it was supposed to contain a quote, which is not true.

Essay coach Sara Nolan says the worst quotes to use in essays are those anonymous ones you might find on a mug or greeting card.

A quote by Abraham Lincoln, Thomas Jefferson or Martin Luther King, Jr., almost always stops the flow and leaves me cold. I believe famous quotes zap the personal feel of a narrative essay.

On some level, they send the message that you don't have enough to say about yourself. And I find myself not trusting the writer: Would a teenager really care that much about a quote by one of these famous dead guys? Or are they just falling back on what their English teachers wanted them to include in essays?

Have confidence that your own opinions are more valuable in these essays, and are what the admissions counselors want to hear.

Dropping in a quote kills the flow and tone of a narrative essay. If you truly like to quote famous people in everyday life, well then, go for it. To make it feel more relevant and believable, maybe find someone you respect who is still kicking, such as David Sedaris, Elon Musk or Patti Smith.

But if not, trust your own words on this one. That will help keep the tone of your essay current and consistent.

Break Only the Rules You Know

As I said earlier, these essays allow a more casual style and voice. There is more flexibility in what you say and how you say it than in your typical academic essay. If you are writing more like you speak, chances are your essay will break some of the formal rules of the English language.

You might end a sentence with a preposition. Or start a sentence with a conjunction, like "but" or "and" or "or." Or use contractions, such as "can't" or "I'll." Sometimes you just have to quietly split that infinitive if it sounds better.

You might use phrases (sentence fragments) as though they were sentences. Like this. Or that. Sometimes you can even make up words, such as words to describe sounds (onomatopoeia: Boom! Zip. Screeeeech. Drip drip drip.)

But you should recognize when you do this and do it for a reason—mainly to create a more conversational tone or add color. Most students break language rules when they try to write more creatively, such as with their anecdotes. This can work wonders or backfire.

When you read other sample essays, you can spot where students broke the rules. Notice why they did it, and what the effect was. Did it work or not?

No matter what, do not go overboard. And when in doubt, stick with the rules.

Chapter Nine

STAY FIT

A strong essay is lean and mean. If it's bloated with redundant or unrelated language, you will lose your weary reader. Like you would do for any successful journey, bring only what you need.

Here are some great ideas on how to trim your essay so you deliver your main point as concisely and powerfully as possible. In writing, less is almost always more.

 **Chop the Top**

If you start your essay with an anecdote, place the reader as close to the punch of the action or moment (the climax) as possible. After you write out a paragraph or two, and briefly set the scene and describe what happened, you might find it's longer than you want.

With a good anecdote, you want it as short as possible to recreate that moment concisely. Sometimes it's difficult to jump in, so you start with some background sentences or more description of the setting than you need. And that's fine—just get it out on paper. But then go back and trim it down.

One trick is to lop off that first sentence, and see how it reads. Often, you didn't need that first sentence. Sometimes you can even lose the first couple of sentences, and it works fine without any set up.

EXAMPLE (from student Sarah Mandi's sample essay in Chapter 11):

~~Even since I can remember my world has been about donuts. My dad worked his way up Duncan Donuts, and eventually bought a couple franchises. So when I needed a summer job last year, it only made sense that I work at one of his shops. It turns out the work was harder than I imagined.~~ It was only my second day on the job. Decked out in my generic khakis and white polo shirt, oversized apron, visor, and bulky headset, I leaned out the window of the drive-through.

"Thank you. Have a nice day," I said for probably the hundredth time that day; it was only 7 a.m.

 ## Write Long, Then Cut

Most admissions essays have word counts or limits. They limit how long you can go, and some require a minimum of words.

I always encourage students to "write long," and not to worry about the word limit at first. Cutting is a lot easier than adding.

When you are getting out your ideas, some will naturally inspire new ones— so keep writing even if you know it's too much. Then read it back, and hack away the bad parts. Usually your new ideas are better than your first ones.

Of course, it's a good idea to keep an eye on your length as you go, mainly to save yourself extra work. Know that one substantial paragraph (about 4-5 sentences) is about 80 to 100 words.

If you come up short on your word count, read through your points and look for places to insert examples. For instance, if you say you worked in a nursing home as part of a community service project, add a sentence that gives an example of what you did and learned. This way you flesh out your essay with material that actually strengthens your point and not just a bunch of fluff.

But in the end, before you send in that essay to your colleges, make sure you are within the word limit requirements.

First Cut Chunks, Then Sentences, Then Words

When you put on your editor cap, and read your essay critically, look first for entire paragraphs or groups of sentences that you don't need. Either they say the same thing you already said and are redundant, or they don't support the larger point of your essay.

Chop those first. Then go through and do the same for individual sentences. You will be surprised how often we repeat the same point without noticing it.

Once you have the body of the essay in good shape, give it a read for individual words. This is your chance to take out the usual suspects:

- **Unnecessary qualifiers**: very, really, kind of, a lot, many, so...
- **Adverbs**: you don't need most of those –ly words, such as annoyingly, smoothly, longingly, surprisingly…
- **"To be" verbs**: am, is, are, was, were. It's fine to have some, but look for opportunities to replace them with power verbs.
- **Duplicate words**: If you use the same word several times in a sentence or paragraph, try to find a synonym.
- **The wrong words**: Sometimes we pop in a word that isn't quite right. Often you sense it's wrong, but can't think of a different one. Find a better one in the thesaurus or state your point in a new way.
- **Don't over –ing**. Words like discussing, arranging, examining…create a kind of language sludge. Switch words that end in –ing to more active language. Opt for the simple present or past.

Punctuation Red Flag: Make sure that you only have one space instead of two between your sentences. Using two spaces is an almost certain tipoff that an adult had a hand in your essay, since only writers who used to compose on typewriters (anyone over about age 50) would do that.

 **Kill Your Darlings**

This is an old writing rule. Most credit it to author William Faulker. Novelist Stephen King also included it in his famous list of writing tips.

The idea is that you often latch onto an idea that you like, or a certain way you expressed it. In fact, you like it so much, that even when it doesn't support your larger point, you don't want to see it go.

You are so self pleased with your turn of phrase or word choices or some other fancy line that you think it has value even if it doesn't fit with the rest of your essay. Resist the temptation to leave it in. In other words, "Kill your darling" and delete it to death.

Chapter Ten

WRAP IT UP

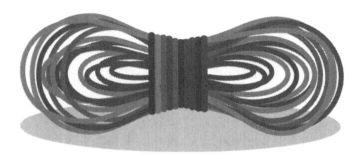

No matter where you set out on a new journey, you usually come home at some point. An effective narrative essay gives the reader that same satisfaction. It takes us somewhere new and exciting, but gently guides us home in the end.

Narrative essays don't necessarily need a formal conclusion, but here are some ideas and tips on how to polish up and end your piece so everyone is happy.

 **Come Full Circle**

Unlike formal essays, you don't always need a conclusion at the end that summarizes what you have said or restates all your main points. But you do want to let the reader know that you are wrapping up.

One way is to link back to your introduction at the end of your essay. If you wrote about an anecdote, try to bring the reader up to the present date on what happened. Give a type of status update.

For example, if you started by describing a time you faced a challenge, let us know how things are going now or today involving that challenge. If you got stuck while climbing the side of a mountain, you could end by saying how you still rock climb but that you now do things differently based on that frightening experience.

Another technique to sign off at the end of a personal essay is to project what you learned into the future. Mention how you will apply the lesson(s) you learned to your life goals and dreams.

This way you will end on some type of broad, upbeat note. If you learned how you needed to prepare thoroughly when doing a risky sport like rock-climbing, you could end with how you expect to keep taking risks in the future, but never without some type of safety net.

Leave With a Kick

While I'm not a big proponent of starting an essay with a single witty grabber sentence, I am a sucker for a one-line "kicker" sentence at the end of a personal essay.

They don't all need one. But it's worth seeing what you can come up with. The conclusion typically will have some talk about your future and lofty, idealistic goals. This is the perfect spot to be earnest and optimistic. One final short sentence can let the reader know that you also have a sense of humor and don't take yourself too seriously.

If you ended your essay talking about the lessons you learned taking risks in rock climbing, and how you expect to apply those to your future goals, you could try to play on that theme for your kicker.

Example: While I'm ready to take the fall for the right idea, I also appreciate the value of a big net. Or: I know I will continue to keep looking up as I strive for my goals, but I will never forget what is below me.

The risk is that they are too corny. At the same time, this is your chance to show your sense of humor and playful side. These are almost like those little comments you throw out when you say goodbye to a group of friends or leave a room—kind of an off-the-cuff comment meant to be an "until next time" closer.

Give it a try. Experiment with word play. You will know if it works or not.

If you don't come up with a kicker, just end with a strong, broad statement that projects into the future.

See if you can find the kickers in the Sample Essays in Chapter 11.

 **Be Your Own Editor**

When you write, you get out your ideas on paper (or computer)—any way you can. When you edit, you read what you wrote and make changes. These are two separate activities, and each takes a different approach.

Writing is fast and messy—you focus on getting out your ideas and don't worry about making them perfect.

Editing is when you slow down and go back and clean it up—you look for problems, find mistakes and make changes.

Be aware of when you are in either mode. Each has its own mindset.

When writing your rough draft, your mindset is anything goes, "it's all good," go, go, go! Give yourself lots of hugs. You can do no wrong.

When you step into your editor role, it's a different voice altogether. Kind of Dr. Jekyll turning into Mr. Hyde. You don't have to beat yourself up, but it's time to get picky. Actively look for problems and ask questions. Be critical.

Demand only the best: Does that paragraph make sense? Is the introduction too long? How can I find a better comparison to make my point clearer? Did I already say that earlier? Boy, I used a lot of adjectives in that sentence.

Pretend someone else wrote your rough draft, and they asked you to review it.

Then make the fixes. Read it out loud to catch parts that are bogged down or where the tone is off. One of the best ways to catch those final errors is to print out your draft and edit it on paper. Mistakes seem to pop out more.

 **Seek the Right Feedback**

It's often a good idea to ask someone to read your drafts, especially your final one. But if you want constructive criticism, you might need to provide the reader with some direction first.

Many parents, teachers, college admissions counselors and other adults will review your essay and give you advice based on what they think makes a good essay. The problem is many of them either have their own agenda (even if they don't realize it), or they don't have a solid grasp on what makes a strong essay these days.

Things have changed in recent years. Colleges want essays that are engaging and personal. Many adults still believe these essays are a student's chance to tout accomplishments and try to impress colleges with pedantic, formal writing. The more stuffy it sounds, the better they think it is.

They are so wrong.

I believe the best way to get what you need from well-meaning adults is to first preface your request with a little background. Before handing it over, tell them that this is a "slice-of-life" essay, which is known to be the most effective, even at the most prestigious schools. Let them know the style is more casual and that you are supposed to sound like a teenager.

Ask for specific points you would like their opinion on:

- Do they think the beginning is interesting and grabs their attention quickly?
- Do you come across as likeable?
- Are there any places where the essay bogged down and lost their interest?
- Are there any parts that are unclear or don't make sense?
- What is the main point they get about you from the essay?
- Can they point out their favorite parts and their least favorite parts?

The hardest part is when an adult will warn you that you "crossed a line" or that you "might want to leave that out." I would listen carefully to their opinion, but use your own judgment in the end. Sometimes these "sensitive" parts are the best stuff. If you are still in doubt, ask a couple other people about it. Maybe you can tone it down a little bit, but not entirely lose the flavor or point you were going after.

Red flag: During the eight years I've worked with students on these essays, I have seen a pattern that concerns me, and I think you should have your radar on for it. Students have shown me college app essays written as assignments for their Language Arts classes that are dull and not very good, but their English teacher gave them an A or high grade. Think about how the criteria for earning a high grade on an English assignment could be different from what college admissions counselors want to see in an essay.

A high grade feels great, and who wouldn't want to just send it in? But the last thing you want is to send in one that's less than stellar. If you have doubts, despite a good grade, get other opinions. Above all, trust yourself!

Try Out a Title

Most essays do not require titles, but I think they are a good idea. It's another chance to give the reader something memorable about you and your piece. If you can only think of a general, dull title, best leave it out. But if you brainstorm a bit, you probably can come up with something catchy.

EXAMPLE: A student wrote an essay about how he broke his wrist playing football, and how he learned more about the game sitting on the bench that season. Theme: How bad things can result in good things/How you learn from a new perspective.

Make a quick list of related words from the essay that you could play around with: break, benched, football, sports, view, injury, hurt, perspective...Let yourself "free associate," which means list key words and sayings that come to mind when you say one of them, such as "break."

Try the word in different tenses, in common phrases, in pop culture phrases (titles of movies, books, songs, etc.) and even clichés can work. Also, skim your essay for catchy phrases that might work. Try mixing up a couple keys words to make your own phrase. You also can use the Internet to brainstorm ideas—just Google your keywords or phrases. Have fun with it:

Breaking Away (movie title)
The Big Break
Breaking Up
Break Out
You Deserve a Break Today (line from McDonald's commercial)
An Unexpected Break
Give Me A Break
A Break from the Past
Beyond the Break

My favorite is Beyond the Break, since it implies the metaphorical movement beyond the injury. But if I didn't like that one, I would move on to another key word.

Keep playing around with them. Make a list. Read them out loud. One word will spark another and so on. You will know almost immediately when you hit on the right one.

If you can't find one you like, just skip it. Better no title than a bad title for your college application essay—unless one is requested or required.

Chapter Eleven

SAMPLE ESSAYS

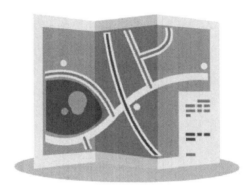

Here are sample narrative-style college application essays from some of my former tutoring students. Most were written in response to one of The Common Application essay prompts. All are personal statements written in a narrative style.

I believe reading what others have written is one of the best ways to understand the style of narrative essays, as well as to find topic ideas.

See if you can see when the writer uses an "anecdote" or real-life story from his or her own experience. Notice what writing techniques they used to craft their anecdote, to engage your interest and get you to care about what they had to say.

Do they set the scene with a few simple phrases that help you see where it took place? Are there any "sensory details" that shape the scene they are describing: What you would see, hear, smell, taste or feel? Check out how they used a little dialogue to bring the moment to life.

Also, go through these essays and try to spot when the writer is showing with an anecdote, concrete details, specific examples, and when they are telling with analysis, reflection or explanation.

Pay attention to those moments in reading these essays when you start to feel something, either a flash of recognition or a moment you really get what they are trying to say. Re-read those parts and try to figure out what exactly caused your reaction.

Did they share something unexpected or something vulnerable about themselves? Did one short sentence help move you through the piece? Was there a kicker at the end that left you satisfied with the essay?

Copy those techniques in your own essay!

If you can tell when the writer is using a certain writing technique, you will be that much closer to learning how to use it yourself.

**Sarah Mandi**
Voorhess, New Jersey
Georgetown University, Washington, D.C.

Donut Domination

It was only my second day on the job. Decked out in my generic khakis and white polo shirt, oversized apron, visor, and bulky headset, I leaned out the window of the drive-through.

"Thank you. Have a nice day," I said for probably the hundredth time that day; it was only 7 a.m.

The line at the Dunkin' Donuts in Atco, New Jersey, continued endlessly out the door; and the drive-through line, even longer. The aroma of sugary donuts and hearty breakfast sandwiches engulfed me as I navigated through the obstacle course of employees, display cases, coffee machines, and ovens. The never-ending line of hungry, impatient customers was starting to fluster me, and I could feel a growing sense of irritation at my poor cash register skills.

Suddenly, in walked my biggest nightmare: a middle-aged man; tall and brooding, his shirt drenched with coffee.

"My coffee lid broke!" shrieked the man, angrily. "You gave me a broken cup! Look what you did!"

I managed to stutter, "I'm sorry," a few times, but I knew that would not cut it. I grabbed a wad of napkins as well as a new cup of coffee, apologizing profusely. A moment later, another customer started to voice her irritation for getting a Boston Creme Donut instead of a Bavarian Creme Donut.

If anyone should know the difference between those two donuts, it should be me. Looking back, donuts have dominated my life for as long as I can remember. But I had no idea that this business was so complicated—and about more than just people indulging in these fried doughballs.

My dad worked his way through engineering school at Dunkin Donuts, eventually switching careers to invest in the Dunkin Donuts' franchise. I cannot even begin to count the number of times I have brought in donuts to school for my birthday instead of bringing cake, like everybody else. What other family has discussions about the new seasonal, "Brownie Batter" donut, or "Arnold Palmer" Coolata? By the time I was in ninth grade, it was already decided where my first real job would be.

As days went by, I worked tirelessly to get the hang of the job. I could not help but think what was wrong with me; taking simple coffee and donut orders could not be this hard. But eventually, it became routine. I would greet the regulars as they walked through the door asking about their weeks while preparing the order I had memorized.

"Good morning Mr. Edwards, how's your summer going? Medium Coffee, cream and sugar today?"

I grew accustomed to the fast-paced environment. I started to recognize instances where throwing in a few extra munchkins to make the customer happy was appropriate. I began to hear the snarky comment from customers, "Oh, you must be new," less and less. The satisfaction from finally being able to complete seemingly trivial tasks was just as great as any sense of accomplishment I had felt before.

I came to the realization that angry customers were not a sign of poor job performance but a part of human nature that I would have to accept and manage. There would always be a mother who got mad when her daughter's donut was missing sprinkles; but such things would always be out of my control. I learned not to be ashamed of making mistakes. Even though I still confused the Bavarian Creme and Boston Creme Donut, I continued to work the counter until I got it right.

I finally understood why my dad had poured his heart and soul into this business. It wasn't just about providing the best food or making the largest profits; it was about providing an experience, taking part in a community, and putting yourself out there. I may never work at a Dunkin Donuts again, but I now understand how it makes people happy—and why that matters.

 **Sophie Funck**
Chicago, Illinois
Santa Clara University, Santa Clara, CA

Fast Doesn't Always Win

As I walked into class, I spotted the two dreadful words on the white board before I even slid into my desk. They could have been in flashing neon lights: "Pop Quiz." Even though I had completed the reading homework, I knew I was sunk. My cheeks grew hot as I tried to ignore my classmates' pencils furiously writing down answers.

"Think, just think," I told myself over and over, trying to conjure the relevant facts and information. Even though I read the exact words in the same book as everyone else, nothing stuck.

Ever since I was old enough to try to memorize facts or read out of textbooks, the information seemed to float right out of my head. I could spend hours reading and re-reading every page of an assignment, but the next morning it was all a vague memory. Looking back, I have always taken the longest to learn anything. I could not read until the second grade. While my friends advanced to chapter books, I was reviewing sight words, over and over again.

Even though my brain insisted on taking its sweet time, I always knew I was smart. I just learned differently. My parents figured that out early on and supported and taught me through my strengths. "Different isn't a bad thing," they would often say. Finally, I was tested and discovered that I have an auditory processing and visual memory disability, which means I take longer to absorb information. Despite the diagnosis, I forced myself to think I was a stellar student because I knew if I worked twice as hard and twice as long as my classmates, I could compete at the highest level.

In grade school and junior high, teachers set homework time limits for me so I wouldn't spend too much time on assignments, but I insisted on finishing the work to prove to myself that I was as capable as my classmates. I was given an assignment and I completed it, no matter what. Even though I was pleased with my grades, the feeling of being "less than" continued to linger in the back of my mind.

Over time, things started to come together. I began to use different tricks and strategies to help me learn more efficiently. In history, one of my most challenging subjects, I would picture facts as stories and print out maps and pictures to help me understand the content. Creating acronyms and singsong rhymes with mnemonic devices and doing multiplication tables with my fingers were still favorite strategies. I also was a master at time management and organization. When I stressed about school, I told myself, "I will get it done," and that "Everything will be ok." These creative learning tools not only helped my approach with school, but with other obstacles in my life.

Ironically, having been a competitive swimmer for 12 years, the focus was about being fast. Fortunately, I learned there was always something more valuable than being fast when it comes to swimming and learning. As I began my senior year, I started to realize that the feelings I had and the pressure I felt were not unusual. I understand now that being fast and mainstream aren't always better; the ability to retain a lot of facts is not the crucial part of learning; and that smart is a highly subjective adjective.

I am at peace with my way of learning. I know that I can compete in a "fast" world because I've done that in high school. But it's more important for me to follow a pace and path that allow for spontaneity, reflection, creative learning and deep thought. My passion for art is a vehicle for this path. I am excited to enjoy the ride and experience a journey that supports and encourages the integration of who I am and how I learn.

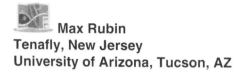 **Max Rubin**
Tenafly, New Jersey
University of Arizona, Tucson, AZ

Pushing Through

When we pulled up to the McDonald's drive-through, my friend ordered the usual for our group: "Four Big Macs, four large fries, and four large Cokes." But at the pick-up window, I poked my head out from the back seat and told the server: "Make that three of everything, please. And add a bottle of water."

"A bottle of water?" My friend turned to me with a baffled look on his face. "Since when? Are you on a diet or something?"

I felt a flush of embarrassment, but I just tried to ignore the comments and change the subject. Not many teenage boys have to watch what they eat. Most of my friends can devour almost anything and stay thin. I thought I was like them and dined on junk food without a second thought until about two years ago. One morning in the beginning of my sophomore year, I stepped on the scale and was shocked to see that I was more than 20 pounds overweight.

I do not remember the exact day when I woke up and decided to start exercising and to change my diet. Life altering decisions usually are not reached in one day. At first, I did not notice my weight gain, but my parents did. My dad tried to get me to work out. My mom tried to make me eat more home-cooked meals. But I did not want to deal with it. In my late middle school and early high school years I was inactive, spending too much time sitting around, playing video games and watching TV. At some point, I started to put together that not only was I heavy, but that I was insecure about my body, and that was also related to my shyness. It was all connected. I was unhappy about myself—and it showed.

When I finally decided to clean up my diet and begin working out, I realized that I knew nothing about either. I started by doing hours of research on nutrition and exercise until I felt confident enough in my knowledge to create a meal plan and exercise regimen for myself. I then joined a gym and started to eat healthier food at home and in school.

When I first began working out it was excruciatingly difficult and painful. Each day I would wake up after a workout from the previous day and barely be able to get out of bed. It felt as if the muscles I was using had never been used before. As weeks passed, I noticed significant changes in my physical appearance; people around me also noticed. I stopped feeling insecure about my body. My self-esteem improved. I even found it much easier to approach people and make new friends.

Going to the gym four to five times a week, I had to learn how to dig deep and push through the pain. Even when my body was telling me that I could not do anything more, I managed somehow to do more. I learned to apply this method of "pushing through" and persevering to schoolwork. I took more precise and diligent notes. I spent more time doing homework. I participated more in class. I started to prepare for tests far in advance.

When I was younger, my parents and teachers kept telling me something that I thought made little sense: "You can do anything you set your mind to!" After transforming my body, staying dedicated to working out and maintaining a healthy diet, I discovered that they were right. I learned that if I believe in myself and do the hard work, I can achieve whatever I strive for. Now I am confident that whenever something requires dedication, determination, and perseverance, I will "push through" and succeed. And I will keep reaching for a bottle of water over a Big Mac.

 **Emily Walton**
Cincinnati, Ohio
Wake Forest, Winston-Salem, North Carolina

Sap-Stained Hands

As I was in the middle of tugging another prickly Christmas tree out of the stack, I felt a gentle, yet emphatic tap on my shoulder.

"Excuse me, I'm looking for the person who decorated these wreaths," said the insistent shopper.

With a red ribbon in my mouth and sap-stained hands, I turned around hoping to discover Martha Stewart. Instead, I found myself facing a short, elderly woman in a full-length coat with a matching blue hat. According to her church nametag, her name was Ms. Charlotte.

She informed me that as head of her church's Christmas Decorating Committee she was looking for something "Southern and unique." Ms. Charlotte asked for several sample wreaths, and said if they met her approval, she would order 40 more.

The size of the order surprised me. This was my first time working at my grandparents' Christmas tree lot in Burlington, North Carolina, and I felt as though I was just getting the knack for picking out the best trees and keeping up with the festive, though hectic business. I had made some wreaths before, but had yet to try anything beyond the typical style. I told Ms. Charlotte I would have the samples for her by the next morning.

Growing up, our visits to the tree farm had always been about fun. The rows of planted spruces and firs felt like a playground, and my sisters and I held tea parties among them with our stuffed animals. By middle school, I learned that a farm has a job for every age. We sprayed fertilizer, carried tree tags and planted saplings. As the eldest daughter of an only daughter, I was surrounded mainly by uncles and male cousins, each determined to out farm the other. For sport, they enjoyed identifying the farming deficiencies of the three Walton city girls. As the daughter who loved reading or drawing, I was often an easy target.

Last Christmas, I wanted to do more than serve as my cousins' punching bag, and volunteered to work at the family lot. When Ms. Charlotte asked me to design unique wreaths—along with the promise of a large order—I took it as a personal challenge. I may have a quiet side, but when challenged, I have come to appreciate the power of my ability to listen intently, form a strategy and deliver results.

When Ms. Charlotte came back, she inspected my samples and told me they were too ordinary. As she turned to leave, I put aside my hurt and shock and begged for a second chance. She paused, and stated that she would return after dinner.

That afternoon, I alternated between helping customers and designing something new for Ms. Charlotte. Pinecones? Dull. Holly? Old. "Southern and unique." Her words kept taunting me. I was desperate. Ms. Charlotte's rejection only strengthened my determination. I was desperate to prove to her and myself that I could deliver. Then, lightening struck. I combined mixed-green wreaths from Fraser firs with local leaves (blue and yellow cypress with magnolia). Rejecting the traditional Christmas colors, I wove in ribbons of gold and white.

When Ms. Charlotte returned, five wreaths waited for her inspection. I braced for another rejection. Regardless of her reaction, I owed her a debt of gratitude. Ms. Charlotte had pushed me beyond my comfort zone. I had the satisfaction of knowing that I can deliver even at the height of holiday hysteria, and keep my creativity and poise in the process.

After walking down the table touching each of the wreaths, Ms. Charlotte opened her purse and handed me a list containing the wreath order sizes.

"Now, let's talk about what you're going to do for my house," she said, smiling for the first time.

At that moment, I knew then that I too was a Christmas tree farmer, ready to take on the world.

Hasan Jhaveri
Orlando, Florida
University of Virginia, Charlottesville, VA

A Trio of Tolerance

Imagine this: A Hindu boy kneeling down into sujdah with a family on Eid. A Christian family saying grace to bless dinner on Diwali. And me, a Muslim kid covered with a rainbow of colored powder while celebrating Holi alongside Hindu families.

Growing up I thought we were just three boys, much like any others; boys who rode the bus together, who learned to swim together, who climbed 20-foot trees together. Nothing made us happier than running around the neighborhood with one another. Looking back, I realize, our friendship bridged the most longstanding and bitter of obstacles: intolerance. I am a Muslim. Avi is a Hindu. John is a Christian. Since the beginning of our friendship, each of us has been enriched with cultures - different from our own - that formed our individual identities.

Despite these differences we became brothers. Through the time spent at sweltering Orlando soccer practices, open houses, and other school events our parents also became friends, and our families began to meet regularly for dinner, where we all engaged in lively discussions about foreign policy and philosophy.

Over the years our relationships grew and we began to rely on one other. I'd stay up late to teach John complex Calculus concepts and he'd return the favor later with some of his crazy girl advice. Avi and I hammered out our student originals for English class while jogging around the neighborhood. And when my house burned down in 2007, John's family invited us to live with them for a of couple months.

Until recently I hadn't given much thought to the reason we all "clicked" so well, but now I have a theory: We are all moderate and tolerant when it comes to many of our beliefs. It's not that we don't have strong principles and deep passions that shape our identities, but we are confident enough in them and in ourselves that we have room to remain open to radical new ideas.

Today I appreciate how I benefitted by the accepting nature of all these influential people, and how they made me see that religion should be something that bonds us not separates, as all advocate love and respect to others.

Had my parents been traditional Islamic people who only hung out with other Muslims, I may have felt isolated and my friendships might have been limited to cliques of Muslims at our school. Instead, I was open and comfortable with diversity and in return enjoyed a broad group of friends.

Not only am I comfortable discussing Muslim theology, but I can talk with ease about Vishnu and Shiva and verses of Paul to the Philippians. I no longer characterize myself as one religion or one culture but as an open-minded world citizen. I don't just celebrate Eid, I celebrate Christmas and Diwali, too. I teach John cricket and in exchange he teaches me Texas Hold'em. I read Arabic teachings from the Quran while Avi explains why his culture has so many deities.

I understand much of the world is not as welcoming of our differences. But my plan is to stay open and tolerant. Not only does it lead to great friends, it gives me hope. Maybe someday our commonalities will overpower our differences. I believe that's something called peace.

**Raquelle Rubin**
Tenafly, New Jersey
Purchase College, SUNY, Purchase, New York

Better Out Here

The summer before my freshman year of high school, my parents forced me into solitary confinement. They hid my phone and computer. I was not allowed to leave the house. At the age of 13, I thought for sure that my life was over.

My method of coping with my deep self-hatred – intoxication – could no longer be used. The numbness of substances faded and was replaced by the most gruesome, raw emotions. I did not know how to handle the intensity of feeling again; I was overwhelmed and miserable.

This was how I spent the majority of that summer, alone in my bedroom. Everyday I woke with no purpose, no motivation, no yearning to do anything. But then one day, I found an unused notebook in my desk. It changed my life. I began to write, and I have not stopped since.

In the prison of my room, I found myself. At one point, I realized that I must not distract myself from my thoughts and feelings, but rather think about why I felt this self-hatred. It all went back to the spring of my second year in middle school, when I realized that I am a lesbian.

That truly scared me. It wasn't that I feared coming out to my parents or what my friends would think. It was that I just did not wish to be different from others. I felt that this would only cause me anxiety and bring seclusion. I began to have a deep hatred of myself. All I wanted to do was drown out my emotions, and that is exactly what I ended up doing.

I acquainted myself with the wrong crowd and illegal substances. The life I began to lead allowed me to bury my feelings. My grades suffered, and my relationships with those I cared about most deteriorated. Fortunately, my parents noticed all the worrisome things I was doing right before I became a lost cause.

During the long hours in my room, all the thoughts I had went into journal entries, poetry, and short stories. My feelings became my muse. Seeing what I felt put on paper allowed me to understand myself. I did not know why I had such a powerful fear. Every time I wrote a poem about my sadness and my anger at being gay, my feelings about myself improved.

Defining my emotions helped me analyze the situation more thoroughly and clearly. I realized that being gay was not a terrible thing; quite on the contrary, I recognized that this difference of mine gave me a unique perspective on interrelations among people and enabled me to appreciate and accept the differences in others more readily. Ultimately, I was able to accept myself and face the world.

Now, as Founder and President of the Gay-Straight Alliance in my high school, I am devoted to helping LGBT students to accept their sexuality, and to encouraging heterosexual students to accept people who are not "straight." The GSA is there to provide support, advice, and information. Every week we discuss an issue that targets the LGBT community, and we discuss the various sexualities that people have. I specifically tell members first to accept who they are before trying to accept others' differences. I try to show them that they can be loved no matter what, whether gay, straight, bisexual, or anything else.

For many, my best advice is this: "Spend a lot of time by yourself and take a hard look at the issue that you are having trouble coming to terms with. If you can, write about it, or find some outlet for those feelings." Hopefully, this will lead them to self-acceptance and in turn give them the ability to step out of their rooms, out of their shame and fear, and face the world. It's a lot better out here!

 **Andreas Strandgaard**
Denmark
New York University Shanghai, Shanghai, China

My Own Parent

Standing on the stage, I looked out on the small audience of parents. It was fifth grade, and I was playing a cop. It wasn't the lead role, but I was proud because my mom had promised to come. But as time went on, I realized she wouldn't be able to make it. While I was looking down on my friends' happy and proud parents clapping and cheering, I could feel my eyes slowly filling with water and my muscles tensing.

Sadness changed to anger and anger evolved to a disbelief in my parents' appreciation of me. As I could feel my emotions getting out of control, I cleared my mind and swallowed the negative emotions as I had done so many times before. Regaining my composure, I bowed for the applause, and no one noticed.

Just before I was born, my parents decided to leave the comfort of a day job and become self-employed management consultants. Without the safety of a monthly paycheck, they both had to work and travel much to pay the bills.

To my brother and me, this meant we often had to move around between different families, depending on who had room and time. On the good days, we stayed with our grandparents. On the best days, we slept over at a friend's house and on the rest of the days; we stayed with co-workers and other friends of the family.

In the beginning, being away from my parents that much was tough. I would often wake up in the middle of the night not knowing where the window, door or light switch was. Disoriented and frightened by the dark, I stumbled around trying to find any light source to help me. Even with my brother around, situations like these would often leave me feeling sad and lonely.

I never thought about it before, but now I believe that in the absence of my parents in those moments, I became one for myself. Instead of feeling down, I rationalized the situation and suppressed my emotions with logic and reasoning, just like an adult. I taught myself to do my homework on my own and go to bed on time, and with the help of my grandparents, I learned how to cook food, and wash and iron my clothes.

Although it could be difficult at times, I realize today how valuable those experiences have been, and how privileged I have been having so many people helping to provide for me. All those years spent with different families have provided me with unique opportunities to learn about life, people and dreams. And in the end, each and every one of those people and experiences have shaped me into becoming someone with healthy values and firm principles— someone that I am proud to be.

Probably, the biggest lesson I learned is how big an impact it can have on people to make them feel appreciated and respected and how little it actually takes to achieve that. It makes me proud to be the one who always turns up and being that someone who tries his best to look beyond what first meets the eye and make everyone feel noticed.

Today, my dad is 66 years old, but he is nowhere retiring. My parents still work tirelessly, and they will continue to do so for many years to come. While I occasionally still miss having quality family time, their passion for their job and desire to improve the lives of others through their work have become a major inspiration for me. Whenever I need encouragement to work hard towards my ambitions of becoming an inspiring leader and doing what I can to support others in their path to success, I now look to them to find it.

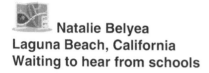 **Natalie Belyea**
Laguna Beach, California
Waiting to hear from schools

Caring for Myself

Lying motionless, my body tensed up as I could hear the careful, yet quick unwrapping of needles. A sweet older Chinese woman in a physician's coat methodically shuffled through the dim room. The supposedly soothing oriental music of bamboo flutes and wind-like percussion only heightened my pulse. An uneasy rush of panic engulfed my body.

"Don't worry; you won't feel a thing," Dr. Lily offered. "One, two, three."

"Okay. I'm ready," I responded while shaking.

"Natalie, the needle's already in!"

As someone who regularly fainted at the mere sight of needles, I never dreamed that one hundred acupuncture needles would be piercing my legs, back, and hands. Having explored all mainstream medical options, my orthopedist proposed acupuncture to combat the chronic pain stemming from my fractured back.

I fractured my lower back in eighth grade playing competitive club volleyball. I pushed my body to an extreme with multiple weekly practices, ignoring the constant stabbing pain in my back. What started out as tolerable evolved to where I had trouble walking as numbness and pain radiated down my legs. Doctors tried everything to avoid surgery—five MRI scans, three CTs, five back braces, physical therapy, epidurals, and trigger point injections.

School proved the hardest, sitting through seven hours of classroom lectures. Sophomore year, the school administration recommended that I drop my advanced classes or pursue home schooling, but I refused to allow my injury to deter me.

Apart from the stiff and unsupportive chairs, I'm most comfortable at school. I honestly love it. Academics have served as a distraction to help me cope with the pain. I could not comprehend abandoning my love of learning; however, I could not continue in pain. As a result, I withdrew from the final classes of my sophomore year, photography and honors pre-calculus, to shorten my day and to stay in school.

Luckily, my orthopedist suggested acupuncture during my sophomore year. I remembered initially comparing acupuncture to a voodoo ritual, but now I thrive from its benefits. I have since pursued other forms of alternative medicine with the most recent being the Egoscue Method, a form of physical therapy that focuses on posture. Some of these methods worked; others did not. Consequently, I am now able to manage my pain through mainly physical therapy, a lumbar support cushion, and medication.

Today, I'm doing great—not perfect—but I've learned how to manage the pain. Dealing with a fracture that two percent of those who possess it don't heal from, I've learned to become more open minded to alternative forms of medicine and other ways of thinking. Spending hours resting my back, I've had much time to think and have subsequently realized how meaningful a sweet card from my grandparents or a call from a friend has meant to me. In learning to care for myself, I have also learned to think and to care for others more.

Although I would never wish such pain on anybody, I'd be a different person, if this had never happened. Through learning about my injury and body, I have become more cognizant of my priorities and abilities. It revealed my strength in dealing with pain and overcoming my fear of medical procedures. I have learned the importance of being open because without it I could still be confined to bed. Going through such a difficult ordeal granted me a zeal for life and an appreciation for the seemingly insignificant.

While I still have a fractured back, I am immensely appreciative for what my injury has taught me about being open to others, new opportunities, and myself. I am elated to partake in the new possibilities that college and life will offer.

 **Alex Knoll**
Maplewood, New Jersey
Waiting to hear from schools

A Matter of Principle

I asked my mom again, but the answer was still no. I sighed and thought, "A simple no hasn't stopped me before, and I won't let it stop me now."

As much as I like to be an obedient son, I couldn't help but take this as a challenge. My mind was already starting to whirl with ideas. I thought long and hard, but nothing seemed feasible at first. However, MacGyver said it best when he told his partner, "When it comes down to me against a situation, I don't like the situation to win."

Although I'm not the hero that MacGyver was, and I certainly don't have a television show, I do feel the same way about solving problems. So, when my parents decided I shouldn't have a T.V. in my room, I didn't raise a white flag of surrender. This wasn't about watching my favorite television shows; it was a matter of principle.

Just like MacGyver, I like to use materials from around my house and garage to come up with innovative solutions. In the same way he uses things like paperclips and string, I use scraps of wood, household items, and hot glue. When an idea hits me, I can't wait to go to my garage workbench, turn on the radio, and get to work.

One day, a light bulb went on in my head when I saw a mini projector in a high-end catalog. I ordered it online. I dug through my dad's wood scraps and pulled out the three pieces I needed. Then, I fastened them together with screws and nuts and in less than an hour I had a multi-jointed, movable arm.

A few days later my package arrived. I rushed to my room, secured the wooden arm to my bed's headboard, and mounted my brand new, palm-sized projector to the end. The trickiest part was gathering the necessary cables and converters: an HDMI cable from the "electronics drawer" in the basement, a charging cable from an old phone, and the audio cable from an unused speaker. Ready to go, I hooked it all up to my iPhone, crossed my fingers and threw the switch.

As I lay on my bed, streaming Netflix on the wall, I admired my work. But the feeling was short-lived as I almost immediately thought to myself, "What will my parents think?" My inventions hadn't always gone over so well in the past. I once built a Ping-Pong ball catapult, which seemed like a flawless idea on paper but it badly cut my hand when it exploded under the pressure of an inordinate number of rubber bands. I made an iPhone dock with what turned out to be expensive CDs. I had to pay to replace them.

It was inevitable; my parents would surely discover what I had created. I just hoped they would be open-minded when they did. Fortunately, they were more than okay with it, sitting on my bed with me to watch a movie! I'm lucky that they appreciate how much I love to build and improve things.

There is a certain undeniable satisfaction that comes from overcoming a challenge intelligently, cleverly, and creatively using my brain and bare hands. I've discovered that more than half of the fun is the actual project; it's like a puzzle when I have to figure out how to build something with the tools and materials that I have available. This extends to other areas besides gadgets, including my fascination with the ideas that build great businesses.

Despite my interest in building, I don't see myself as an engineer or an architect. As a future business major, and later an entrepreneur, I already have a pretty good idea of how I'll be spending most of my time: give me a problem to solve and stand back. It's a matter of principle!

 **Kaylie Monahan**
Irvine, California
University of Colorado, Boulder

Over It

Wearing my turquoise-and-red beaded sandals, a braided headband wrapped around my forehead, tan fringy shorts, and an oversized brown shirt emblazoned with a multi-colored tribal symbol, I stepped out of my mom's car filled with confidence and joy.

My dark, freshly curled hair blew in the warm summer air, and as I marched up to meet my friends, I smiled and flashed a peace sign for fun.

"Who dressed you today?" said one of my friends, giving me the up and down inspection.

As I fumbled for a reply, I suddenly realized that other people were looking at me, and not the type of looks that most people want. I was shocked and frankly, embarrassed by my rude friend. Most kids would have run home to change. But I just adjusted my headband so the feathers showed better, lifted my head high, threw back my shoulders and headed for the nearest store. They didn't appreciate my bohemian outfit. Too bad for them, I was over it.

When I reflect to that unforgettable day, I laugh to myself. For a sixth grader, I am proud that I had developed my independent style, and was determined to be myself. Weirdly, a couple of years later, I discovered that the popular Bohemian Indie Store, Urban Outfitters, was actually reflecting my diverse fashion style.

Before I knew it, I found myself halfway through junior year shopping at thrift stores, and attending fashion and sewing classes at the Fashion Institute of Design & Merchandising. These opportunities shaped my personality through wearing and making clothes, and as a result it opened my mind to the power of taking risks in fashion-no matter the response from others.

I have always been that person who wears outrageous clothes that most people could not rock. To me, it is all about trying, and being confident no matter the outcome. It's not that I don't consider my audience. I just don't let what they think dictate what I do or wear.

Currently, I describe my style as Boho-Native American. I am not exactly sure why I am attracted to this trend, but it may be because of my grandmother. She was part Native American and was comfortable wearing clunky turquoise jewelry and bold, earthy prints. Although everyone in my family was not a huge fan of her cultural fashion, I valued how she always took risks, and never cared what people thought of her.

Through my experiences, I believe that in any career the key to success occurs when you make an impact on society. In life, as much as I like to look good, I also like to take risks when it comes to fashion. Fashion displays a separation between society, and myself and precludes restrictions. I am interested in business, and I feel that the components of successful businesswomen are: strong-willed, risk-taking, independent thinkers, intelligent, organized, and hardworking.

I'm not sure of what my future holds, however, whether it's in fashion, business, or both, I am going to keep being myself, taking risks, chasing my dreams, and remembering what a wise man once said, "Do you want to spend the rest of your life selling sugared water or do you want a chance to change the world?"

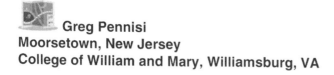 **Greg Pennisi**
Moorsetown, New Jersey
College of William and Mary, Williamsburg, VA

Lucid Dreamer

Standing among towering redwood trees, I wondered if they would look even more incredible from above. The next moment, I felt my feet rise above the ground, and began accelerating upward until I was hovering above the forest's canopy.

This is just one example of many lucid dreams I've had. This ability to become aware of my dreams, and control what happens in them, first appeared when I was seven years old. Over the years, my imagination became my only limit – as long as I was asleep.

I've zip-lined through a Siberian prison complex, tasked with rescuing a double agent. I've given birth to sprawling mountain ranges with the flick of a wrist. I've even orchestrated my own rendition of the Big Bang.

After years of adventuring through these controlled dreams, I've found my favorite pastime. It's an extremely peaceful scene: a pond, about the size of three swimming pools, nestled at the bottom of a small, thickly wooded valley. Dark trees sprout up from the hills in every direction. A thick layer of fog floats overhead, acting as a cover to the giant bowl of a valley. Below the water's surface, silhouettes of impossibly giant fish move in slow, graceful circles.

That's it. No super powers or crazy adventures. Only me, sitting by this lake with these fish in the middle of the woods. Who would have known that if I could have anything I wanted – from the ability to fly, to exploring the cosmos – this would be my choice. I'm almost surprised at myself, and I can't help but consider what this says about me in my waking life.

When I'm sitting in this beautiful place, I am at peace. Sometimes, I'll give myself a guitar to play, an activity that I enjoy both in dreams and real life. Other times,

I'll sit at the lake's center and admire the behemoths swimming beneath me (liquids become appropriate walking surfaces, given the right attitude).

What's interesting is that I'm not at all like this in real life; I don't consider myself to be spiritual or meditative. In my free time, I'm typically itching to organize plans, or doing something physical to keep myself occupied. Because of this contrast, I began questioning why this lake was my favorite place to be. After all, in every lucid dream I have, I elect to go there and sit as opposed to flying, or creating new solar systems.

After much thought, I began to realize that I simply enjoy the peace. When I'm there, I'm happy; I wouldn't want anything more in my real life than what I have at that lake. What's exciting about this is that it's completely attainable.

I began to think about how my goal in life is happiness. I've always seen anger as inefficient; subsequently, I usually elect to keep a cool head. Freaking out has never really done anyone any good. This runs parallel to my dreams; I decide the best way to react, and then make it happen.

While thinking about my fondness of this serene lake, I also realized that everything I truly enjoy is surprisingly simple; my favorite pastime is playing my guitar. When I play, I go into autopilot. After playing certain songs for years, I'll let my fingers do the work while my mind is let free to wander. I also enjoy memorization; I once memorized thirty digits of pi for a school contest. Then another seventy because somebody told me I couldn't. Then another fifty while on a five-hour flight.

I haven't decided which direction to head in with my real life, or what career path to pursue. It's not as if I lack goals or dreams, rather that I want to make the best decision. Ultimately, though, happiness remains my endgame. And like that spot by the lake, I know I just have to decide to make it a reality.

Chapter Twelve

MORE HELPFUL GEAR

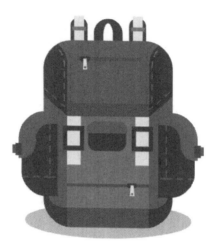

 Best Books on How to Write:

Bird By Bird, Anne Lamott

Crafting the Personal Essay, Dinty W. Moore

Escape Essay Hell: A Step-By-Step Guide to Writing Narrative College App Essays, Janine Robinson

Narrative Writing, George Hillocks, Jr.

Story Craft, Jack Hart

To Show and To Tell, Phillip Lopate

Writing Tools: 50 Essential Strategies for Every Writer, Roy Peter Clark

Favorite College Application Essay Collections:

Heavenly Essays: 50 Narrative College Application Essays That Worked, Janine Robinson

The Berkeley Book of College Essays, compiled by Janet Huseby

50 Successful Harvard Application Essays, compiled by staff of the Harvard Crimson

 Best Books on College Admission:

40 Colleges That Change Lives, Loren Pope

Harvard Schmarvard: Getting Beyond the Ivy League to the College that is Best for You, Jay Mathews

The Best 379 Colleges, 2015, Princeton Review

The College Solution, A Guide for Everyone Looking for the Right School at the Right Price, Lynn O'Shaughnessy

The Gatekeepers, Jacques Steinberg

Where You Go Is Not Who You'll Be, Frank Bruni

College Application Essay and other Internet Resources:

College Confidential: A student-centric, forum-based **college resource** (look under College Admissions for essay-related help): www.CollegeConfidential.com

An online **thesaurus**: www.thesaurus.com.

Big Future (by The College Board), helpful site with information on college app essays: www.bigfuture.collegeboard.org/get-in/essays.

College Board: College planning and preparation tools: www.CollegeBoard.com.

Sample College Essays, "Top 78 Essays That Worked," a nice collection sample essays: www.apstudynotes.org/essays/.

College Prowler: College reviews written by students (great source for essay supps that want to know why you are a fit): www.CollegeProwler.com.

Essay Hell, the hottest resources for writing college application essays. www.essayhell.com.

Essay Hell on Pinterest: Essay Writing help for visual learner at Essay Hell's Pinterest page: https://www.pinterest.com/essay_hell/

Grammarly, an online editing tool (grammar, spelling, vocab., etc.): www.Grammarly.com

Huff Post College Admissions: Online news and features about the college application process, including essays. www.huffingtonpost.com/news/college-admissions/

Teen Ink, sample college essays sponsored by The Princeton Review: www.teenink.com/college_guide/college_essays/

The Common Application, a non-profit which streamlines and manages college applications for more than 500 colleges and universities: www.commonapp.org

The Universal College Application, another application site that accepts about 50 colleges and universities: www.universalcollegeapp.com.

Zoomita: Free essay organizer site, find prompts for essays and supplements from most colleges and universities: www.Zoomita.com.

Chapter Thirteen

GLOSSARY

Common terms used in the writing of college application essays:

Anecdote: A writing technique that succinctly conveys a real-life moment or incident using a narrative style.

Conclusion: The end of the essay, usually referring to the last paragraph.

Copyediting: The process of proofreading an essay to catch errors with spelling, punctuation, word choice, syntax, grammar and overall accuracy.

Core Essay: These are the main essays required by college applications, and are usually about 400-700 words and involve personal statement topics.

Deadline: This is the date when college applications, including the college application essays, are due.

Dialogue: This is when a person's words in conversation are conveyed using quotation marks and attributions (who said what).

Five-paragraph Essay: This is the traditional style essay taught in most junior high and high school language arts classes for expository, personal and other essays.

Grabber: This is used to describe a sentence or two at the beginning of an essay that engages the reader at the outset. Also called "The hook."

Introduction: This is the start of an essay, and usually involves the first paragraph, and sometimes the first couple paragraphs.

Kicker: This is a sentence or two at the end of an essay that tries to leave a lasting impression on the reader.

Lede or Lead: This describes the opening paragraph of an essay (or article, news story or book chapter). The news industry spells is "lede," and its pronunciation rhymes with "need." A strong "lede" engages the reader.

Metaphor: When one thing is compared to another as if they were the same thing.

Mundane Topic: A college essay topic that involves everyday themes.

Narrative essay: A style of essay that uses a story-telling format and style.

Outline: This is a logical plan that writers use to map out and organize the structure of a piece of writing, such as an essay. Some are more intricate than others.

Personal Essay: A first-person essay that is about the writer.

Personal Statement: A first-person essay that tries to describe the essence of the writer—who they are and what they care about.

Prompts: These are usually questions that are asked in college application for students to address in their college application essays.

Sample Essays: These are true-life essays that students wrote for their college applications, and college-bound students read to learn how to write their own.

Self-Editing: This is the process of reading drafts of an essay in progress and looking for ways to improve it.

Sensory Details: These are specific details that writers use in essay to describe the five senses.

Simile: This is a comparison between two items that use the words "like" or "as."

Storytelling: This is when writing includes the conventions of a "story," which include a character or characters and "conflict." Something happens to someone.

Supplemental Essays: These are the additional, and usually shorter, essays that colleges often require students to write in additional their main or "<u>core</u>" essay. They often ask about extracurricular activities or ucational goals.

The Common Application: This is the non-profit organization that facilitates the college application process for most colleges and universities in the

United States. It currently requires applicants to submit one college application essay that responds to one of five prompts, and is 650 words.

The Universal Application: This is like The Common Application, in that this group streamlines the college application process for colleges and universities in the U.S., but has far fewer participating schools, currently less than 50.

The Hook: This is the sentence or two at the start of an essay that tries to engage the reader at the onset. Also called the "grabber."

Thesaurus: A book of synonyms. You can look up one word and find others with similar meanings.

Title: This is what you name your essay using a short phrase and is usually short and memorable. They are not usually required, but a good one can enhance an essay.

Topic: This can be what a student's college application essay is about or its central theme or subject.

Universal Truth: Most essays contain a life lesson that extends to all humans. Examples: You don't always get what you want. No pain, no gain. Love hurts.

Word Count: This is how many words a college or university requires for the length of its college application essays. Many schools list a minimum and maximum number.

Chapter Fourteen

ABOUT YOUR GUIDE

Besides working as a college admissions writing coach, Janine Robinson is a former journalist, freelance writer, teacher and editor who lives in Laguna Beach, California. For the last eight years, she has worked with college-bound students on their college application essays. Janine writes the popular blog, www.EssayHell.com, which is filled with advice, tips and inspiration on how to write these dreaded essays.

For the last two decades, Janine has worked for top newspapers, magazines and Internet companies as both a writer and editor. She worked as a staff reporter on The Miami Herald and Orange County Register newspapers, edited a monthly lifestyle magazine for women, and worked as a writer and editor for several Internet-based education and news sites. Janine also is a credentialed high school English teacher.

Janine has written several other helpful guides for students and others working on college application essays: Escape Essay Hell, which is a step-by-step guide to writing narrative essays; Essay Hell's 2015-16 Prompts Primer, which offers strategies on how to answer the most common prompts; and Heavenly Essays, an inspiring collection of sample essays written by students. All are available as Kindle ebooks or paperback on Amazon.

ACKNOWLEDGMENTS

I think I have the coolest book covers, especially in the cerebral world of college admissions. Laguna Beach graphic designer and artist, Russell Pierce, has created all the images for my blog and books. He is so creative and captured the playful vibe of my essay messages and services.

I'm also indebted to a fellow college application essay writing coach who lives on the other side of the country. Even though she was just about to deliver her first child, educator and essay coach Sara Nolan of Essay Intensive in New York City spent hours combing through this Writing Survival Guide, and not only caught numerous errors, but she gave me great ideas on how to improve it.

I'm most grateful to all the students—from all over the world—who have so generously allowed me to share their college application essays in this guide and my other books. I love how they had the determination and courage to look into their pasts and their hearts and share such powerful, inspiring stories.

Needless to say, I would be toast if I didn't have the support of my encouraging, patient and always kind husband, Charlie. And my two "children," Cassidy (a recent graduate of Hendrix College in Arkansas, who is pursuing a Masters in Teaching at the University of California, Irvine) and Caden (a recent graduate of The University of Puget Sound in Washington, who is earning a degree in chemical engineering at Washington University in St. Louis) continue to show me why it's so important to trust that they will find their own way.

And so will you!

THE END
www.EssayHell.com

Made in the USA
San Bernardino, CA
10 November 2015